KB135038

Great Debates
in Philosophy

Great Debates in Philosophy

Seungbae Park, Ph.D.

Ulsan National Institute of Science and Technology

Preface

This book exposes readers to influential concepts, theories, arguments, criticisms, and replies in philosophy. The essence of philosophy, I believe, lies in rigorous argumentations over fundamental and general issues. Being engaged in such argumentations will improve readers' creativity and critical thinking. After reading this book, you will better be able to analyze, attack, or defend positions. This intellectual skill is of utmost importance not only in philosophy but also in science.

Throughout this book, I present philosophical materials in the following four steps. First, I ask a question that I hope will stimulate my readers' curiosity. Second, I answer the question with a theory. Understanding the theory would be both boring and grueling without first being exposed to the question. Third, I present an argument to support the theory. Philosophers do not merely state a position: They try to justify it with evidence and reason. Fourth, I reveal a problem with the argument or a counterexample to it.

Here is an example. Step 1: Thales, the father of Western philosophy, asked: What is everything in the world made out of? Step 2: He claimed that everything in the universe is made out of water. If water undergoes a certain change, it can be transformed into a tree, into a stone, and so forth. A tree and a stone are water in different forms. Step 3: Why should we believe that everything is made up of water? Thales says that everything is solid, liquid or gaseous. Water can be in any of the three states. Therefore, everything is made out of water. Step 4: Iron and air can also be solid, liquid, or gaseous. Why not claim that everything is made of iron or air? Also, is the mind also made out of water?

This book is filled with such well-known philosophical arguments and criticisms against them. I chose most of them from lecture notes that I used for classes at the University of Arizona, the University of Maryland, and Ulsan National Institute of Science and Technology.

I thank all of my students who challenged me to explain this material more clearly. I am also grateful to Professor Richard Healey and Professor Alvin Goldman. They molded my philosophical thinking while I was a graduate student at the University of Arizona.

Seungbae Park

CONTENTS

CHAPTER 03 Ethics

CHAPTER 04 Philosophy of Mind

CHAPTER 05 Epistemology

CHAPTER 06 Evolutions

CHAPTER 07 Personal Identity

CHAPTER

01

Basic Terms and Logic

In this chapter, we go over some basic terms widely used in philosophy. Learning them is the first step in constructing a rigorous philosophical argument.

1. Philosophy

Philosophy can be roughly defined as an attempt to answer general and fundamental questions. What is a general question? A question about organisms, for example, is more general than a question about animals because there are organisms that are not animals, viz., plants. A question about animals is more general than a question about mammals because there are animals that are not mammals such as reptiles and insects. What is a fundamental question? A question about whether God exists or not is more fundamental than a question about whether God loves human beings or not. The latter is built upon the former. If the former collapses, so does the latter.

It is, however, difficult to draw a clear-cut line between philosophical and non-philosophical questions. It is not clear exactly how general a question should be in order to be regarded as philosophical. Nor is it clear how fundamental a question should be in order to be counted as philosophical. In any event, philosophers are interested in highly general or fundamental questions.

Our rough definition of philosophy would not be satisfactory to those who are new to philosophy. It does not tell them very much about what philosophy is. This is not surprising. Knowing philosophy, I believe, is like knowing the taste of an apple. The only way to know the taste of an apple is to eat one. Defining the word 'apple' does not help very much. Likewise, defining the word 'philosophy' does not help very much. The only way to know philosophy is to engage in rigorous philosophical debates.

Fields of philosophy can be divided according to a variety of criteria. For instance, it can be divided between Eastern philosophy and Western philosophy. Eastern philosophy can be subdivided into Chinese and Indian. Western philosophy can be subdivided into Anglo-American philosophy and Continental philosophy. If the criterion is time, there are ancient, medieval, modern, and contemporary philosophies. If the criterion is the object of our investigation, there are metaphysics (the study of reality), epistemology (the study of knowledge), and axiology (the study of value). There are also philosophy of mind, philosophy of language, philosophy of religion, philosophy of art, social and political philosophy, philosophy of science, philosophy of education, and the philosophy of law.

Philosophers raise and answer three kinds of questions: metaphysical, epistemological, and axiological. Any question of the form "Does X exist?" is metaphysical. X might be God, dinosaurs, electrons, justice, mind, and the like. Any question of the form "How do you know that X exists?" is epistemological. Again, X might be God, dinosaurs, electrons, justice, mind, and anything else. Any question of the form "Is X good?" is axiological. X might be a human being, human behavior, rules of human behavior, social conventions, or government policies. Philosophers of science, for example, ask: Were there dinosaurs? How does DNA look like? These are metaphysical questions. How do we know that there were dinosaurs? How do you know that DNA has the structure of double helix? These are epistemological questions. Scientists sometimes discard data when they clash with the theory. A philosopher of science may ask, "Is it good or bad for scientists to stick to a theory despite the observational evidence to the contrary?" This is an axiological question.

2. Belief

I have many beliefs: the Earth is round, God exists, water is H_2O, and the sky is blue. But what is a belief? Where is it? Consider my belief that the sky is blue. Does this belief exist in the sky or in my mind? It exists in my mind. It follows that a belief is a mental state. It is something that exists in the mind. It depends on our mind for its existence, so if there were no mind, there would be no belief. Since a belief is a mental state, it is not made up of atoms. Contrast a belief with an apple. An apple is a physical object, and is made up of atoms. A belief is not.

There are many kinds of mental states: pain, itch, hunger, thirst, belief, wish, hope, love, loneliness, sorrow, depression, elation, disposition, and excitement. But a belief possesses a characteristic that sets it apart from other mental states. Unlike other mental states, it is true or false. The belief that the Earth is round is true. The belief that the Earth is flat is false. Contrast a belief with a pain. A pain is not a kind of mental state that can be true or false. Suppose that your finger is cut and that you feel pain. It does not make sense that the pain is true or false. Hope is not a kind of mental state that can be true or false either. Suppose that you hope that you become a teacher. It does not make sense either that your hope is true or false. A hope can only be fulfilled or unfulfilled. So a belief is a mental state that is capable of being true or false.

3. Truth

Under what condition is a belief true? What do true beliefs have in common? What do false beliefs have in common? Consider the following beliefs:

(1) The Earth is round.
(2) The Earth is flat.
(3) There is a life outside of the Earth.
(4) There is no life outside of the Earth.

(1) is true, and (2) is false. Why is (1) true? One answer is that (1) is true because we have sufficient evidence for it. A problem with this answer is that there is no proof whether (3) is true or (4) is true. Yet, either (3) or (4) is true. We only do not know which one. So truth is one thing; evidence is another. A statement might be true even if we do not have evidence for it. A statement might be false even if we do have evidence for it.

According to Aristotle, (1) is true because it corresponds to a fact; (2) is false because it does not. A fact in this context is a state of affairs. It is a piece of the world to which a true belief corresponds. For any true belief, something in the world renders it true. That thing is a fact.

Mind(Subject)	World(Object)
belief$_1$ ⟶	fact$_1$
belief$_2$ ⟶	fact$_2$
belief$_3$ ⟶	fact$_3$

On the one hand, a belief is a truth-bearer, that which bears the property of being true or false. It is mind-dependent in that if there were no mind, the belief could not exist. A fact, on the other hand, is a truth-maker, that which makes a belief true. It is mind-independent in that it exists whether the mind perceives it or not. There seems to be a causal relationship between a belief and a fact. The fact is the cause, and the belief is the effect. I would not form the belief, for example, that a cat is on the mat, if a cat were not on the mat. In addition to beliefs, there are other truth-bearers: claims, sentences, statements, propositions, opinions, theories, and views. In addition to facts, there are other truth-makers: events and states of affairs.

Aristotle's theory of truth is called the correspondence theory of truth. It states that a belief is true if and only if it corresponds to a fact. That is, a true belief corresponds to a fact, and a belief corresponding to a fact is true. (1) is true because it corresponds to a fact, i.e., the world is as (1) says it is. It is a correct description of the world. It matches up with the world. (2) is false because the world is not as (2) says it is. It is an incorrect description of the world. It does not match up with the world. So truth consists in correspondence with the world. In the case of (3) and (4), we do not know which one corresponds to a fact.

Let me report two classic objections against the correspondence theory of truth. First, it does not handle mathematical statements, i.e., it fails to explain why a mathematical statement is true. Consider 1+1=2. It is true that 1+1=2. But why is it true? To what does the true statement correspond?

$$1+1=2 \qquad \blacktriangleright \quad ?$$

Is there a mathematical fact that renders this mathematical statement true? If so, where is it? What does its truth-maker look like? It is not clear whether there is a mathematical fact in the world that purports to make a mathematical statement true. Thus, the correspondence theory cannot handle mathematical statements.

Second, perhaps, there are facts in the world that correspond to the sentences like 'The Earth is round' and 'It is raining.' But how about the sentences like 'The Earth is not flat' and 'It is raining or not raining'? Those statements are true. But why are they true? To what do these statements correspond?

The Earth is not flat. ──────────▶ ?

It is raining or not raining. ──────────▶ ?

Are there facts in the world that correspond to these statements? If there are, what do they look like? It is not clear whether they exist or not. Thus, truth cannot be equated with the correspondence to a fact.

4. Argument

Philosophical and scientific activities consist of constructing and destroying arguments. An argument is a collection of statements some of which are intended as premises and one of which is intended as the conclusion. A premise is a statement provided to support the conclusion. It is the evidence intended to show that the conclusion is true. Consider the following example:

> A white mouse and a human being are physiologically similar.
> A new drug worked on a white mouse
> ∴ It will also work on a human being.

The first two statements are premises, and the last one is the conclusion. The first two statements support or justify the conclusion. Thus, to ask for an argument is to ask for a justification.

Philosophers strive to construct good arguments to persuade their audience of their views. It follows that where there is no argument, there is no philosophy. In philosophy, we are interested in what evidence we can come up with to justify a claim. Merely stating a claim or proffering an opinion is not philosophy. This is also true of science. Scientists do not merely state a theory about the world. They justify it either by performing experiments or by connecting it with other established theories. Experimental data and other established theories are premises; the theory that they support is the conclusion. Einstein's general theory of relativity predicted that the apparent positions of stars should change during a solar eclipse. The prediction was ascertained by observational evidence. The observational data are premises, and the general theory of relativity is the conclusion. So presenting an argument is a way to discover truth.

5. Deduction vs. Induction

In an argument, the premises might support the conclusion with 100% probability. Consider the following argument:

All of UNIST students are smart.
John is a UNIST student.
∴ John is smart.

In this argument, the conclusion necessarily follows from the premises. Put differently, if the premises are true, the conclusion must be true. There is no possibility at all that the conclusion is false, if the premises are true. Such argument is deductively valid. In a deductively valid argument, the content of the conclusion does not go beyond the content of the premises, i.e., the conclusion does not say more than what the premises say. The information in the conclusion is already in the premises.

In an argument, premises might support the conclusion with less than 100% probability. Consider the following argument:

Most of UNIST students are smart.
John is a UNIST student.
∴John is smart.

In this argument, the conclusion probably follows from the premises. Put differently, if the premises are true, it is likely that the conclusion is true. There is a possibility that the conclusion is false, even if the premises are true. Such argument is inductively correct. In an inductively correct argument, the content of the conclusion goes beyond the content of the premises, i.e., the conclusion says more than what the premises say. The information in the conclusion is not present in the premises.

6. Fallacies

A fallacy is an error in reasoning or a flawed argument. We should do our best to avoid fallacies. Let's investigate some fallacies that are common in intellectual debate.

6.1. Ad Hominem

Ad hominem is an attack on the author of an argument instead of on the argument. Consider the following example:

> Plato: Mathematical objects like circles and triangles are more real than physical objects like cups and trees.
> Goethe: Plato's theory is false because he was a homosexual.

In this example, Goethe committed *ad hominem* because he attacked not Plato's position but Plato himself. Consider another example:

> A: I believe that the motion of molecules is responsible for heat

because if two pieces of cold metal are rubbed together at high speed, they become hot.

B: Your theory is objectionable because you hope that your new theory will make you rich and famous.

B committed *ad hominem* because his criticism is leveled not at the argument for the kinetic theory of heat but at its proponent. Instead of criticizing A's argument, B tried to discredit A's theory by questioning A's motives.

A proper response to a person who commits *ad hominem* is to point out that morally bad people might be correct in their beliefs. Serial killers, for example, could believe that the Earth is round. Scientist might have the selfish motive to become famous with their new theory. However, it is one thing to have a questionable motive; it is another to have a false theory. Thus, pointing out that a person is bad does not to refute that person's argument. What is required to refute an argument is the evidence against it.

A lesson can be learned from *ad hominem*. In an intellectual debate, we should always separate the idea from the person who initiated it. It is permissible to criticize the idea, but not the person. Asking a personal question is inappropriate because that is the first step toward the fallacy. Suppose that you and your opponents have a debate over the legalization of drugs, and you ask your opponents whether they are drug users or not. Such a question can be taken as an attempt to discredit your adversaries, not their arguments for the legalization of drugs.

6.2. The Straw Man

The straw man fallacy occurs when we criticize our opponent's position after distorting, exaggerating, stretching, or misunderstanding it. We attacked not our opponent's position but what we take to be our opponent's position, and our opponent's position is different from what we believe to be our opponent's position. Consider the following example:

> Darwin: Species have evolved by natural selection. All terrestrial organisms have descended from a common ancestor.

> Critic: Your theory is false because humans have not evolved from monkeys.

The critic misinterpreted Darwin's position and then criticized that misinterpreted version of Darwin's position. Darwin never claimed that humans evolved from monkeys. Instead, he claimed that humans and monkeys have evolved from a common ancestor called hominids and that hominids are a species different from humans and monkeys.

When people commit the straw man fallacy in a debate, they only waste their time and offend their opponents. The opponents will only say "I didn't say that! Why would I make such a stupid claim?" In order to avoid this fallacy, we have to analyze our opponents' argument thoughtfully and correctly before criticizing it. If our opponents' argument is not clear, we ought to ask for clarification. If this is not possible for some reason, we should interpret their position favorably, assuming that they would not make a foolish claim that we can easily refute.

When we write a paper, we criticize our opponent's position. When we do so, we might have to quote our opponents as follows:

> I must point out, however, that it is not part of extensional realism that the mere difference between scientists' arguments for past theories and their arguments for present theories is enough to avert the pessimistic induction. (Park, 2016: 52)

If we do not quote our opponents' sentences, but merely summarize or paraphrase them, our readers may suspect that we committed the straw man fallacy.

6.3. The Appeal to Ignorance

In an appeal to ignorance, a premise states that there is no evidence for something, but the conclusion makes a definite claim. The following examples are all appeals to ignorance:

There is no evidence that God does not exist.
∴ God exists.

There is no evidence that God exists.

∴ God does not exist.

There is no evidence that you are not a communist.
∴ You are a communist.

All these arguments are fallacious. The conclusion does not even probably follow from the premise. A reasonable thing to do after we declare that there is no evidence is to suspend judgment, not to jump to a conclusion. After all, nothing follows from ignorance.

On whom does the burden of proof fall? It falls on the person who makes a claim. If a prosecutor claims that a defendant is guilty, the prosecutor should provide proof, not the defense attorney or the judge. The prosecutor cannot ask the defense attorney to prove that the accused is not guilty. Similarly, if theists believe that God exists, they should prove that God exists. They cannot ask their opponents to prove that God does not exist. Also, if atheists do not believe that God exists, they should prove that God does not exist. They cannot ask their adversaries to prove that God exists.

An appeal to ignorance is distinct from an argument whose premise is questionable. In an appeal to ignorance, a premise states explicitly that there is no evidence for something, that we do not have the information for something, or that we do not know about something. But an unjustified premise does not make such an assertion. Consider the following argument:

There are hostile aliens.

∴ We should be prepared for an attack by aliens.

There is insufficient evidence for the premise, but the premise does not say that there is no sufficient evidence for the belief that there are hostile aliens. It follows that this argument is not an appeal to ignorance. The same goes for the following argument:

God exists.

∴ We should go to church.

There is insufficient evidence for the premise, but no appeal is made to ignorance in the premise. Hence, the argument about the existence of God is not an appeal to ignorance. With regard to this kind of arguments, we can only say that there is no justification for the premise, so we do not have to accept the conclusion.

6.4. Begging the Question

To beg the question is to assume the truth of a claim in dispute in an attempt to prove it. In other words, begging the question arises when a premise presupposes the truth of the conclusion.

Begging the Question

To beg the question is to assume the truth of a claim in dispute in an attempt to prove it.

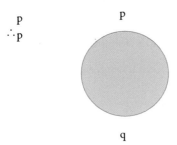

Suppose, for example, that two thieves worked together, and stole three gold rings. One thief takes two of them, triggering the following exchange with the other thief:

> Thief 1: Why do you take two gold rings?
> Thief 2: Because I am your boss.
> Thief 1: But why are you my boss?
> Thief 2: Because I have two gold rings!(Copi and Cohen, 2009:156)

In this exchange, the claim under dispute is that Thief$_2$ is entitled to two gold rings because Thief$_1$ disagrees with it but Thief$_2$ agrees with it. Let us call it p. When p is challenged, Thief$_2$ uses q (He is the boss) to justify it. However, when q is challenged, Thief$_2$ uses p to justify it. This amounts to using p to justify p itself. Thus, Thief$_2$ commits the fallacy of begging the question, assuming that p is true in the attempt to prove it. The premise that Thief$_2$ is the boss presupposes that Thief$_2$ is entitled to two gold rings, which is under dispute. Begging the question has no persuasive force. Thief$_1$ who originally found p unconvincing is still not convinced of p after the exchange with Thief$_2$.

The name 'begging the question' comes from the idea that the question in a debate is the issue that is in dispute, and to beg the question is to ask that the very matter in controversy should be conceded. Sometimes, begging the question is called a circular argument.

A large circle may go unnoticed.

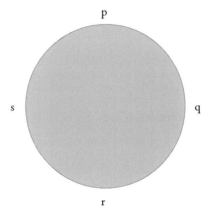

In an intellectual debate, a circle may be so large that the circularity may go unnoticed, and even great thinkers are sometimes guilty of it.

For another example, suppose that a theist claims that whatever the Bible says is true, triggering the following exchange with an atheist.

Theist: Whatever the Bible says is true.

Atheist: Why do you think so?

Theist: Because the Bible says whatever it says is true.

The theist is begging the question. When p (Whatever the Bible says is true) is challenged, the theist uses *p* to justify itself. In other words, when the atheist challenged the Bible, the theist appealed to the Bible to justify it. Such an argument cannot change an opponent's mind. When the Bible is challenged, it is pointless to appeal to the Bible for justification. The following exchange also involves the fallacy of begging the question:

A: How can she afford that nice car?

B: Because she is rich.

A: Why is she rich?

B: Because she can afford that nice car.

In this dialogue, B committed the fallacy of begging the question, failing to answer B's question of how she can afford the nice car.

In an intellectual debate, your opponent may accuse you of begging the question. If you have begged the question, then you should try to come up with a different premise to justify the point under dispute.

A caveat is in order. Just because an argument begs the question does not mean that the conclusion of that argument is false. All it means is that the conclusion is not justified. There might be good evidence for the conclusion, but we just have not found it yet. In the three examples above, there might be other reasons for thinking why Thief 2 is entitled to two rings, why whatever the Bible says is true, and why she can afford the nice car. When our opponent commits the fallacy of begging the question, we ought to withhold judgment as to whether the conclusion is true or false.

6.5. The Slippery Slope

Antiabortionists might run the following argument against abortion. If we legalize the abortion of a one-month-old embryo, we should also legalize the abortion of a two-month embryo because we cannot draw a line between the one-month embryo and a two-month embryo, i.e., because no justification can be given for the position that the abortion of a one-month-embryo is permissible, but the abortion of a two-month embryo is not. Now, if we legalize the abortion of a two-month embryo, we should also legalize the abortion of a three-month embryo for the same reason, and ultimately we should legalize the abortion of a ten-month-old fetus. However, aborting a ten-month fetus is clearly problematic, given that it looks so much like a born baby. Therefore, the abortion of a one-month embryo should not be legalized. This argument is an example of the fallacy of the slippery slope.

How can the fallacy of the slippery slope be formulated? We have a chain of events: a, b, c⋯z. If a is allowed, b should be allowed too. If b is allowed, so should be c, and ultimately z. However, z is a disastrous event. For that reason, a should not be allowed. To speak figuratively, we should not give our enemy an inch because if we do it, they will eventually take a mile. The term slippery slope comes from the idea that you cannot stop once you are on it.

How should we respond to the fallacy of the slippery slope? My response to it is that we are justified in drawing an arbitrary line along the continuum as long as there are clearly problematic and unproblematic cases, and insofar as we are better off with the arbitrary line. For example, the speeds at which a car can move are in a continuum. It is clearly dangerous to travel at 150km/h in downtown traffic, but it is clearly unproblematic to travel at 50km/h an hour. In such a situation, we should draw a line, say 80km/h, and pass a law saying that if you drive faster than 80km/h, you will be fined. Admittedly, the choice of the line is arbitrary. No justification can be given for why we should draw the line at 80km/h as opposed to 79km/h or 81km/h. Even so, we should draw the arbitrary line because we are better off with it.

It would be nice if events are not in a continuum, but they are. They are will be with us forever just like our shadows. Hence, we should learn to live with them. If we are afraid of them too much, then we cannot even enact a law at all, and we should flout all the existing laws. Thus, if we do not want to live in a lawless society, we should not let the fallacy of the slippery slope run around and undermine our social system.

Study Questions

1. What is a belief? Where is it? What is its characteristic that sets it apart from other mental states?

2. State and criticize Aristotle's correspondence theory of truth.

3. What is an argument? Give its definition and provide an example.

4. Are the following arguments deductively valid or inductively correct?

   You and I are physically similar to each other.
   I feel pain when my finger is cut.
   ∴ You would feel pain if your finger is cut.

   If Jill and Jack love each other, they will get married.
   If they get married, they will have a baby.
   ∴ If they love each other, they will have a baby.

5. Provide definitions and examples of the following fallacies: *ad hominem*, the straw man fallacy, appeal to ignorance, begging the question, and slippery slope.

CHAPTER

02

Philosophy of Religion

Does God exist? If so, what is the evidence? If not, what is the evidence? In this chapter, we critically examine several arguments for and against the existence of God as defined by Christianity.

1. The Argument from the First Cause

A popular version of the argument from the first cause goes as follows: I was created by my parents, my parents were created by their parents. Ultimately, God is the starting point of the chain of creations. Thomas Aquinas's (1225-1274) version of the argument from the first cause can be summarized in the following form:

> Every event has a cause.
> The chain of causes must stop.
> ∴ The first cause existed.

The first premise seems to be true. Look at events and things around us. Nothing happens without a cause. Things cannot bring themselves into existence. Suppose, for example, that a car breaks down. We may not know what caused it to break down but the cause is there to be discovered.

The second premise also seems to be true. An infinite regress is not satisfactory because it is impossible that an infinite amount of time has already passed. Only a finite amount of time could have passed. So without the starting point of time, there could not be the present.

The two premises seem to support the conclusion that the first cause existed. The first cause is alleged to be God. God was not created by something else. But he caused other causes. He created everything else. Without God, there would be nothing. God is the starting point of everything in the universe.

There are a few of objections to the argument. Let me start with the most prominent one. What caused God? Who created God? Theists might answer that God does not have a creator. God was there from the beginning. David Hume (1779/1947) objects that we can say the same about the physical universe. If the chain of causes must stop, why not stop at the physical universe? Why stop at God? In other words, theists posit that everything has a cause except God. By contrast, Hume postulates that everything has a cause except the universe.

Another objection against the argument from the first cause is that it establishes at best the existence of the first cause. It does not establish the existence of God, who is supposed to have created the universe, and who is supposed be all-powerful, all-knowing, and all-good. It is one thing that the first cause exists; it is quite another that God exists. In other words, there is no guarantee that the first cause is God.

According to atomism, an atom has a shape, size, and mass. It moves about in empty space in accordance with laws of nature. It is tiny, invisible, indivisible, uncreatable, indestructible, and eternal. Notice that an atom is eternal. If an atom is eternal, so is the universe. Hence, it has neither beginning nor end. So if atomism is true, there is no such thing as the first cause. Of course, atomism might be false. But so might be theists' belief that God exists.

A mystery springs from the assertion that God created the universe. Where was God before he created the universe? An existence always involves a location. After all, it does not make sense to say that something exists, but it exists nowhere. So God must have existed somewhere before he created the universe. But it is not clear where he existed. Also, how old was God when he created the universe? According to the Big Bang theory, spacetime was created along with the big bang which happened approximately fourteen billon years ago. Hence, there was no time before the big bang event.

2. The Argument from Design

Imagine that you came across a watch on a heath. Given that it is a complicated thing, you would immediately infer that an intelligent being made it. After all, a random physical process cannot create a complicated thing. It is implausible that a wind blew on a lump of matter and transformed it into a watch. The best explanation of the watch is that it was created by an intelligent designer, a human being. Likewise, it is unlikely that nature worked on a lump of matter and transformed it into a human being, a complicated thing. The best explanation of a human being is that he was created by an intelligent designer. The intelligent designer is God. So claims William Paley (1743-1805). His argument from design for the existence of God can be summarized as follows:

A human being and a watch are similar in that they are both complex.
The watch was made by an intelligent designer (=a human being).

∴The human being was also made by an intelligent designer (=God).

The first premise seems to be true. A watch has many parts. They are intricately connected to keep and display the time. A human body also consists of many parts working closely together to serve the purpose of sustaining life. For example, my eyes enable me to see a refrigerator. I walk to the refrigerator, grab the milk with my hand, and drink it. My eyes, legs, and hands function together to keep me alive.

An immediate objection against the argument from design is that the intelligent designer must be complex like other complex things in the universe. So there must be a higher intelligent designer who created the intelligent designer. Now, given that the higher intelligent designer is complex too, he must have been created by a super-higher intelligent designer. Thus, we need an infinite number of intelligent designers to explain the existence of human beings.

Second, there are many religions in the world, each with its own god. Which god is the intelligent designer who created human beings? There is no guarantee that the intelligent designer is the divine being as defined by Christianity or by any other religions. So even if the argument from design is successful, it does not establish the existence of God. In other words, it is one thing that the intelligent designer exists; it is another that God exists.

Third, there is no guarantee that there is only one intelligent designer who created human beings. There might be several intelligent designers who worked together to create the complex biological organisms. So the argument from design, even if successful, does not necessarily lead to the existence of God as theists would have us believe.

Fourth, some complex things are bad. For example, cancer cells and HIV are complex and bad. They must have been created by an intelligent designer. A problem is that God is thought to be benevolent. It is not clear why the benevolent being created such things that cause suffering.

Finally, Darwin's evolutionary theory claims that life began as single-celled organisms and that organisms have evolved by natural selection from a simple form into a complex form. Evolutionary theory obviates the need to invoke an intelligent designer to explain why there are complex organisms.

Theists could reply that organisms were simple when God created them, but they evolved and later became complex. God created all the evolutionary processes in which simple organisms became complex. Thus, evolutionary theory is compatible with the argument from design, i.e., they can stand together.

The preceding reply might be tempting to theists. On close examination, however, it clashes with what the Bible says. The Bible says that God created a human being in his image. The theory of evolution says, however, that human beings have evolved from single-celled organisms. It is not clear how we could reconcile what the Bible says with what the theory of evolution says. It appears that evolutionary theory and the Bible cannot go hand in hand. If one is right, the other is wrong about the origin of human beings.

3. The Argument from Miracles

Suppose that a sea is parted, that the sun comes to a standstill, and that five loaves of bread and two fishes fill the stomachs of five thousand hungry people. We are tempted to think that God worked a miracle. A miracle is an event that is contrary to a law of nature. God can violate a law of nature, given that he is all-powerful. Thus, the occurrence of miracles is an indication of the existence of God.

A standard objection against the argument from miracles is that it is not clear why God would break his own law of nature. An all-powerful being could have created a perfect law of nature. Why did God create an imperfect law and then break it? Paradoxically, the occurrence of miracles undercuts the view that God is all-powerful.

Theists might retort that human beings cannot know what God has in mind when he makes a miracle. God's idea is forever beyond the human ken. Atheists reply, however, that theists are human beings too, so they cannot know what God has in mind. This implies that we cannot know what God thinks. God is reputed to love human beings. But we cannot know that God loves human beings? Accordingly, theists' appeal to ignorance has a disastrous consequence on their own beliefs about God.

Hume (1779/1947) exposes another problem with the argument from miracles, viz., we can never know that a miracle occurred. People once thought that solar eclipses and the appearance of comets were miracles. Science revealed the true causes of those phenomena. We no longer think of them as miracles. We do not invoke God to explain them. We can construct an inductive argument against the argument from miracles. The history of science has ample instances in which science has explained putative miracles that were initially attributed to God. So when an inexplicable event occurs, it is reasonable to think that science will eventually explain it. Consequently, we are advised to suspend our judgment as to whether a miracle occurred until science unveils its true cause.

4. The Argument from Religious Experiences

We have five senses: visual, auditory, tactile, olfactory, and gustatory. They enable us to perceive, but they do not reveal everything to us. There is an aspect of reality that we cannot perceive with the five senses. For example, our eyes cannot see ultraviolet and infrared rays. Some people claim that they have seen God and even talked with him. They go further, saying that they have an enhanced sixth called the sixth sense that allows them to see things, including God, that ordinary people cannot see. Therefore, God exists.

Should we accept this argument from religious experiences? Suppose, for example, that I *see* a book on the table. How can I be sure that there is a book on the table? First, other people can see the book too. I can even take a picture of it. In this sense, the book is public. Second, I can *touch* the book. I can pick it up and drop it. I hear a sound when it hits the table. The tactile and the auditory sensations support the visual belief that there is a book on the table.

Therefore, I can be sure that there is a book on the table.

In contrast, the same cannot be done about the belief that God exists. What religious people allege to have perceived with the enhanced sense is private. They cannot share the object of their perception. Moreover, it is not clear how the five senses can support their religious experience. Until the sixth sense is proved to be reliable, we may have to withhold our judgment about their testimony that they have perceived God with the enhanced sense.

Furthermore, how can we recognize God? Suppose that you lived a life of self-abnegation for one hundred days, meditating alone in a temple on a mountain. On the one hundredth day, you have a religious experience in which a man appears and tells you that he is God. The experience seems so real that you believe that God exists. It is not clear, however, whether you can know that the object of your religious experience is God or not. Of course, he says that he is. It does not follow, however, that he really is. Even if the word 'God' is inscribed on his forehead, he might not be God. So how can you be sure that the object of your religious experience is God?

The situation gets worse when people of different religions claim to have perceived their gods. Christians, Muslims, Buddhists, and Greeks claim, respectively, that they have seen God, Allah, Buddha, and Zeus. There is no way to resolve this dispute. The five senses cannot be the court of appeal in this case because they cannot prove that the sixth sense is a reliable source of knowledge.

5. The Problem of Evil

5.1. The Content

Evil exists. Evil is such things as murder, rape, robbery, cancer, AIDS, tornado, earthquake, flood, and famine. They cause sufferings to human beings. Christianity attributes to God three properties: omnipotence, omniscience, and benevolence. In plain English, God is thought to be all-powerful, all-knowing, and all-good. So what? Since God is all-powerful, he can prevent and eliminate evil. Since he is all-knowing, he knows that evil exists. Since he is all-good, he has the will to prevent and eliminate evil. If so, why does evil exist? It seems that God as defined by Christianity does not exist. This is called the problem of evil. Several positions are available to theists in relation to the problem. I will introduce four of them here.

5.2. The Grand Plan

Stephen Wykstra (1984) argues that God knows why evil exists but human beings cannot. God is an infinite being, whereas we are finite beings. A finite being cannot know what an infinite being has in mind. To use an analogy, a nurse gives a child a flu shot, the child experiences the pain, and he thinks that the nurse is evil. He does not understand why she gave him the pain. In contrast, the nurse knows why he experiences the pain. She has a great reason for giving the shot, viz., to protect the child from illness. Likewise, we do not understand why evil exists, but God does. God has a great plan with evil. We just do not know what it is.

Atheists could reply that only God knows whether he exists or not, and whether he has a grand plan with evil or not. Theists cannot know whether God exists or not, and whether he has a grand plan with evil or not, because we are finite beings. Therefore, theists are not entitled to say that God exists and that God has a grand plan with evil. A moral is that it is self-defeating for theists to emphasize that we are finite beings.

Atheists can also point out that Wykstra is guilty of the fallacy of the appeal to ignorance (Chapter 1, Section 6.3.). His argument can be summarized as follows:

> We do not know what God has in mind with evil.
> ∴ God has a grand plan with evil.

It is wrong to believe that God exists after declaring that we do not know what God has in mind with evil. If you declared that you do not know that something is the case, you should withhold your judgment instead of jumping to the conclusion that something is the case. Nothing follows from the fact that we do not know that something is the case. An appeal to ignorance gets us nowhere.

5.3. Moral Growth

John Hick (1966) argues that evil is needed for our moral and spiritual growth. Suppose that a mother gives birth, the baby dies, and the mother grieves. She gets pregnant again, and this time she has a healthy baby. She sheds tears of joy, and fully appreciates the value of the second child. In this story, the first child's death was evil, but it improved the mother's character in that she now appreciates how valuable the second child is. So evil helps us to build our character.

Let me point out two problems with Hick's response to the problem of evil. First, there would be no moral and spiritual improvement in heaven, given that there is no evil there. It follows that heaven is not a good place to be. Second, it is not clear that the value of moral growth outweighs the suffering. It is not clear, for example, that the mother's moral improvement is more valuable than the first child's life. Even if the value of the moral growth is greater than the life, it is not clear why God created the world in which the first child dies and the mother appreciates the second child. After all, he has the ability to create the world in which the first child is alive and at the same time the mother appreciates the value of the second child. It is not clear why God uses the bad means (the first child's death) to justify the good end (the mother's moral growth). Why not use only a good means to achieve a good end?

5.4. Free Will

Theists could say that human freedom is the cause of evil. Human beings are free to do evil as well as good. God only respects human free will. He created evil so that human beings choose to do right things over wrong things. But we sometimes do bad things. For example, a rapist exercises his free will and commits a rape. So it is human beings, not God, that are responsible for the existence of evil. We should not blame God for the existence of evil.

Let's call the preceding response to the problem of evil the free will defense. Perhaps, the free will defense is the best response to the problem of evil from the theist perspective. But there are a few problems with it. Let's discuss them one by one.

An immediate objection to the free will defense is that it is not convincing to those who lost their family members and friends to evil. Suppose that a serial killer murdered your family member. God watched the serial killer killing your family member. But he did not do anything to stop the serial killer. He only respected the serial killer's free will. Can you convince yourself that God is benevolent and that it was right for him to respect the serial killer's free will?

Second, we should distinguish between human evil and natural evil. Human evil is such things as rape, murder, and robbery. Natural evil is such things as earthquake, famine, drought, flood, and volcanic eruptions. The human evil might be the product of free will, but natural evil is not. The free will defense does not explain away the existence of natural evil.

Third, we might not have free will. For instance, God is all-knowing, so he already knows everything that I am going to do. I am like a train which only runs on railroad tracks. Suppose, for example, that I drank milk at 8 o'clock this morning when I was thirsty. It appears that I exercised my free will and drank milk. God, however, already knew that I would drink milk at 8 o'clock this morning even before I was born, which means that it was 100% probable that I would drink milk and that it was 0% probable that I would not drink milk at 8 o'clock this morning. In other words, the former event was bound to occur, and the latter event was bound not to occur. It follows that I had no choice but to drink milk, and I could not have chosen not to drink milk. Since I could not have done otherwise, I did not have free will when I drank milk at 8 o'clock this morning. Therefore, free will is an illusion.

Medieval philosophers like Boethius (1962) and Ockham (1983) were bedeviled by this problem. On the one hand, they wanted to believe that God knew everything even before he created the universe. On the other hand, they wanted to believe that we had free will. Unfortunately, we cannot believe both things at the same time. Efforts need to be made to resolve the conflict between God's foreknowledge and human free will.

5.5. Abandoning One of the Three Properties

Theists might say that God is not all-powerful, but he is all-knowing and all-good. So he cannot destroy evil, although he knows that it exists, and he has the will to get rid of it. He has no choice but to watch evil cause suffering.

Atheists would object that if God cannot eliminate evil, he cannot create the universe either. After all, creating the universe is a much more daunting task than terminating evil. It follows that we should not thank God for having created the universe. If God cannot destroy evil, we should not waste the time worshiping such a weak being.

Theists might now say that God is all-powerful and all-knowing, but he is not all-good. He can defeat evil and knows that evil exists, but he does not care about human suffering. It is for this reason that evil exists. Therefore, we can still believe that God exists.

6. Reason vs. Faith

We have so far examined the arguments for and against the existence of God. The arguments for the existence of God fail to show that God exists. The argument against the existence of God stands. Rational argumentations over God militate against theism. There does not seem to be much of the rational ground for theists to stand on.

In the face of this gloomy situation, theists might say that religion is a realm of faith, not of reason. Reason applies only to science. It does not apply to religion. So reason cannot be used to criticize the belief that God exists. It is also wrong to use it to prove that God exists. The existence of God and the belief in him go well beyond the realm of rational argumentations, so we should throw out all the rational argumentations over God, and we should take a leap of faith to believe that God exists. We should blindly believe whatever the Bible says.

A problem is that faith produces conflicting religious beliefs. By the leap of faith, Christians believe that God exists. They blindly believe whatever the Bible says. By the same leap of faith, Muslims believe that Allah exists. They blindly believe whatever the Koran says. It is impossible for both sides to be right. So faith sometime produces a false belief.

Faith is appealed to not only in the formation of a religious belief but also in the maintenance of it. Holding the belief in God in the face of all sorts of objections against it is regarded as having faith and regarded as praiseworthy. Giving up the belief in God is considered as losing faith and regarded as blameworthy.

Atheists, however, might play the opposite game, i.e., they maintain their belief that God does not exist, come what may. Theists present a strong argument for the existence of God. Atheists adhere to their belief that God does not exist. They are maintaining what might be called paith, which is the opposite of faith. They claim that having paith is praiseworthy and losing paith is blameworthy. Thus, atheists dogmatically believe that God does not exist.

It is controversial whether a dogmatic attitude is rational or irrational. Even scientists sometimes take a dogmatic attitude their favorite theory, no matter what happens in the laboratory. For example, Nicolaus Copernicus (1473-1543) kept his belief that the sun is at the center of the universe and that the Earth moves around it, even though he could not observe the stellar parallax. If the heliocentric theory is true, the stellar parallax should be observable. But he could not observe the stellar parallax because he did not have a telescope. On what conditions are scientists justified to be dogmatic about their theory? This is a thorny issue in philosophy of science which lies beyond the scope of this book.

Consider also that we form many beliefs on insufficient evidence. For example, we tend to think too much of ourselves. In psychology, this cognitive bias is called illusory superiority bias. We might believe, for example, that we drive or look better than average people. But we do not have good evidence for such beliefs. Then, what is wrong with believing or disbelieving in God on insufficient evidence? Furthermore, our life will be miserable if we are constantly reminded that we drive or look worse than average people. Truth is painful. Happiness is more important than truth. This consideration leads us to Pascal's Wager.

7. Pascal's Wager

Blaise Pascal (1623-1662) admits that there is no good evidence that God exists. Nevertheless, he thinks that we should believe in God because there is a chance that he exists. If we believe in God and he exists, we will go to heaven. If we believe in God and he does not exist, we have nothing to lose. But if we do not believe in God and he exists, we will suffer from eternal damnation in hell. If we do not believe in God and he does not exist, we have nothing to gain. Therefore, to believe in God is in our best interest.

This kind of justification for a belief is called practical justification. We are practically justified in believing something when the belief brings about happiness. Suppose, for example, that you are asked to believe that the Earth is flat on condition that you will be given a million dollars. Then, you are practically justified in believing that the Earth is flat. Practical justification is in contrast with epistemic justification. We are epistemically justified in believing something when we possess sufficient evidence that it is true. We do not have sufficient evidence that the Earth is flat. So we are not epistemically justified in believing that the Earth is flat.

What should we do when we are asked to believe that the Earth is flat on condition that we will be given a million dollars? Given that we have the right to pursue happiness, we should take the money, and believe that the Earth is flat. It does not follow, however, that it is true that the Earth is flat. Believing that the Earth is flat does not make it true that the Earth is flat. Likewise, the belief in God may take us to heaven. So we may believe that God exists. It does not follow, however, that it is true that God exists. Our believing that God exists does not make it true that God exists. It is one thing that a belief is useful; it is another that it is true. A useful belief might be false. Pascal's Wager shows at best that the belief in God is useful, not that it is true.

Should we believe in God and live a religious life, as Pascal tells us? What we normally do is in part a function of how *significant* a probability is that an event will occur. For example, if there is a significant probability that it will rain tomorrow, we cancel tomorrow's picnic. But if the probability is slight, we do not cancel it. Similarly, if there is a significant probability that God exists, we should go to church and spend time worshiping him. But if the probability is slight, worshiping God is a waste of time and energy. So the issue boils down to whether there is a significant or a slight probability that God exists. In order to estimate the probability, we should assess the arguments for and against the existence of God. Pascal admits, however, that all of the arguments for the existence of God are bad. It follows that he should believe that the probability that God exists is ignorable and that he should not act on the negligible probability.

Pascal might retort that we insure a house even when there is a low probability that a fire will burn it down. No significant possibility is required to pay the insurance fee because the house's burning down would be a grave loss. Analogously, the eternal bliss that we will get if God exists is so great that the mere possibility that God exists is enough to motivate us to believe in God and live a religious life. Moreover, churchgoers have nothing to lose even if God does not exist because they make friends in church and enjoy worshiping God. In other words, there is an intrinsic value in living a religious life. So believing in God is like insuring a house without paying a fee.

Atheists might argue that we should reject Pascal's Wager altogether because it terrorizes nonbelievers in order to make them believe that God exists. It is primitive, savage, and base to use the threat of punishment to persuade others.

Unfortunately, the foregoing reply is not convincing. The threat of punishment is a prevalent phenomenon in our daily life. We frequently appeal to it when we try to persuade our children, potential criminals, and other countries. Furthermore, we actually impose punishment on them when they are stubborn.

Finally, the reality is not as simple as Pascal depicts. There are many religions in the world, hence many gods that we can choose. Which god should we choose in order to enjoy eternal bliss? Pascal is wrong to suppose that we have only two options: believing in God and not believing in God. We have many options.

In response, Pascal might say that you can choose any god you like. Whichever god you may choose, you are better off if we choose one than if we do not choose one at all. After all, if you choose one, there is a chance, however small it might be, that you will go to a good place after you die, but if you do not choose at all, there is no such chance.

Study Questions

1. State and criticize the argument from the first cause and the argument from design. Do you agree or disagree with them? Why?

2. State and criticize the argument from miracles and the argument from religious experiences. Do you accept or reject them? Why?

3. State the problem of evil. What is evil? Provide an example. Show how the existence of evil undermines the belief that God exists. Explore a possible position a theist could take vis-à-vis the problem of evil, and then defend or attack the position.

4. Assess the attitude of believing something by the leap of faith.

5. State and respond to Pascal's Wager. Should we believe in God and live a religious life, as Pascal tells us?

CHAPTER

03

Ethics

We do many things in daily life. Some of them are moral, while others are immoral. Consider the following examples:

Moral Acts
- Saving a drowning child is right.
- Helping the poor is moral.
- Telling the truth is good.

Immoral Acts
- Murder is wrong.
- Rape is immoral.
- Cheating is bad.

What makes an action moral or immoral? What makes helping the poor and telling the truth moral? Why are murder and cheating immoral? What is the criterion for distinguishing right from wrong acts? Different answers to these questions are given by different ethical theorists. We will examine them in this chapter.

1. The Divine Command Theory

According to the divine command theory, what makes an action right is that God commands it; what makes an action wrong is that God prohibits it. Helping the poor, for example, is right because God approves of it; murder is wrong because God disapproves of it. Thus, God's thinking determines whether an action is right or wrong. Nothing is right or wrong apart from God's will. If there were no God, there would be no right acts and no wrong acts. God creates moral properties and facts. In Plato's dialogue, Socrates asks, "Is an action right because God wills it? Or does God will it because it is right?" (Schick and Vaughn, 2010: 358) The divine command theory gives an affirmative answer to the former question.

John Arthur (1996) raises a difficulty with the divine command theory. Given that God is omnipotent, he should be able to turn an immoral act into a moral act by commanding it. For example, he should be able to make rape a moral act by approving of it. He should also be able to turn a moral act into an immoral act by prohibiting it. For example, he should be able to make saving a drowning child an immoral act by disapproving of it.

This raises an intriguing question. Why does not God make rape a moral act when he can do it? Either he has a reason for not doing so, or he does not. If he does have a reason, we want to know what it is. If he does not, we should not worship him, for he arbitrarily took a position. Suppose that someone says, "I have chosen the position that rape is immoral over the position that rape is moral. My choice was arbitrary. I flipped a coin." We would not respect such a person. By the parity of reasoning, we would not worship God if he does not have the justification for his position that rape is wrong.

Arthur's criticism of the divine command theory is strong. It does not, however, confute the position that God knows better than human beings about what actions are moral and what actions are immoral. For example, he knows, but human beings do not, whether homosexuality is moral or immoral. So if we want to stay moral, we should only do what he says is moral. An act is moral or immoral independently of God's will, and God discovers whether an act is moral or immoral just as humans do. But we should seek divine guidance on moral matters because he is omniscient.

2. Cultural Relativism

According to cultural relativism, cultural approval is what makes an act right, and cultural disapproval is what makes an act wrong. Helping the poor, saving a drowning child, and keeping a promise are right because our culture approves of them. Murder, stealing, and lying are wrong because our culture disapproves of them. So the common feature of all the right actions is that they are commended by our culture, and the common feature of all the wrong actions is that they are condemned by our culture.

Consider, for example, eating beef. Eating beef is right in the US because American culture approves of it. But it is wrong in India because Indian culture disapproves of it. Cultural relativism claims that no culture is better than other cultures. So American culture is no better than Indian culture, and Indian culture is no better than American culture. There is no absolutely right culture. All cultures are on a par with each other. Consequently, cultural relativism bars us from saying, "My culture is better than your culture, so you should discard your way of life and follow my way of life."

Cultural relativism is similar to the theory of relativity (Harman, 2008: 11). Suppose that a car is traveling at 80km/h with respect to the ground. How fast is the driver moving? An answer to this question depends on what the frame of reference is. If it is the ground, the driver is moving at 80km/h. But if it is the car, the driver is not moving at all. An object is in motion or at rest, depending on what the frame of reference is. Likewise, an action is moral or immoral, depending on what the frames of reference. Eating beef is right, if the frame of reference is American culture. It is wrong, if it is Indian culture. Thus, morality is relative to culture. Now, there is no fact of the matter as to which frame of reference is better than others in physics. It is not the case that the car is a better frame of reference than the ground when we measure the velocity of the driver. There is no absolute space against which the absolute velocity of the driver can be measured. Analogously, Indian culture is no better than American culture and vice versa. There is no absolutely good culture against which an action can be said to be absolutely good or bad.

What motivates cultural relativism? Our moral beliefs are shaped and molded by our culture. Indians, for example, believe that it is not permissible to eat beef because they grew up in the culture in which they believe that their ancestors are reincarnated into cows.

Americans, however, believe that it is permissible to eat beef because they grew up in the culture in which cows are treated like other animals, such as pigs and chickens. Different cultures have different moral views.

How can people of different cultures live happily together? Harmony and peace can be achieved through non-interference and mutual respect. A conflict arises when a culture interferes with another by saying, "Your way of life is abnormal and immoral; my way of life is normal and moral." Cultural relativism advises us not to make such remarks, claiming that no culture is better than another. This seems to be an attractive aspect of cultural relativism.

Cultural relativism, however, has the following problems (Schick and Vaughn, 2010: 354). First, consider that the United States had slaves and did not allow women to vote. But now slavery is against the law, and women can vote. So Americans have made moral progress. But if cultural relativism is true, moral progress is impossible. Recall that cultural relativism says that no culture is better than other cultures, which entails that present American culture is no better than past American culture. But moral progress is possible as the examples of slaves and women show. Therefore, cultural relativism is false.

Second, there are conflicting morals views within a culture. Consider that the US is divided into people who are pro-choice and people who are pro-life. American culture approves and disapproves of abortion. So abortion is both right and wrong at the same time, if cultural relativism is true. But one and the same act cannot be right and wrong at the same time. Consequently, cultural relativism is false.

Cultural relativists might retort that the majority opinion is the cultural will. So if the majority of Americans believe that abortion is wrong, then abortion is wrong in the US, and if the majority of Americans believe that abortion is right, then abortion is right in the US.

If the majority opinion is the cultural will, however, then what the majority believe is always true, so it is always wrong for the minority to argue against the majority. But we do not believe that the majority opinion is always true. Moreover, if the majority opinion is the cultural will, conducting an opinion poll is the way to settle a moral dispute. We do not think that the moral dispute over abortion will be resolved if a thorough opinion poll is conducted.

3. Utilitarianism

According to utilitarianism, an act is moral if and only if it maximizes happiness, and an act is immoral if and only if it maximizes unhappiness. For example, it is moral to save a drowning child because it maximizes happiness, and murder is wrong because it maximizes unhappiness:

> Act-utilitarianism, then, says that what makes an action right is that it maximizes happiness, everyone considered. (Schick and Vaughn, 2010: 374)

Thus, the set of moral acts coincides with the set of acts maximizing happiness, i.e., all moral acts maximize happiness, and all acts maximizing happiness are moral. All immoral acts maximize unhappiness, and all acts maximizing unhappiness are immoral. Thus, morality resides in the maximization of happiness. Happiness is the sole factor we should take into account when we morally evaluate a human conduct. Jeremy Bentham (1748-1832) and John Stuart Mill (1806-1873) were utilitarianians.

How would utilitarians go about proving that abortion is right or wrong? Utilitarians might support or oppose abortion. The utilitarians supporting abortion would argue that abortion maximizes happiness. Abortion brings about some unhappiness, but the amount of happiness outweighs the amount of unhappiness. The utilitarians opposing abortion would argue that abortion maximizes unhappiness. Abortion brings about some happiness, but the amount of unhappiness outweighs the amount of happiness. The opposing utilitarians disagree over whether the amount of happiness overweighs that of unhappiness or not, but they agree that the way to resolve the dispute over abortion is to calculate the amount of happiness and the amount of unhappiness that abortion produces.

A classic objection against utilitarianism is that it is difficult to calculate the amount of happiness an action brings about. Happiness is what goes on in our mind. So we cannot quantify it. It is problematic to say that my happiness is 10 units, whereas your happiness is 12 units. Since we cannot accurately measure the amount of happiness, utilitarianism fails to provide a practical guide for distinguishing between moral and immoral acts.

Moreover, we cannot predict the long-term effect of a certain action. For example, should we build a nuclear power plant instead of exploring solar power? The nuclear power plant might yield a quick return, but an accident might occur and nearby areas may have to be sealed off for thousands of years. An action that brings about happiness in the short run may bring about grave unhappiness in the long run:

> Should we take future generations into account when performing the utilitarian calculation? Act-utilitarianism is silent on this point. (Schick and Vaughn, 2010: 376)

To use a plain example, consider the act of saving a drowning child. Utilitarians argue that the act is moral because it maximizes happiness. Critics, however, might object that the child might grow up to become a serial killer. So we cannot know whether it is moral or immoral to save a drowning child.

In my view, the foregoing objection against utilitarianism is a straw man. The straw man fallacy occurs when a criticism against a position is built upon the distortion of the position. Utilitarianism does not claim in that we can *precisely* estimate the amount of happiness, or that we *know* that an action maximizes happiness or unhappiness. It only claims that an action is moral when it maximizes happiness. If we do not have enough evidence to conclude that an action maximizes happiness or unhappiness, so much the worse for us, but not for utilitarianism. We do not have to dismiss utilitarianism.

Suppose that your daughter is beaten and raped. As a result of her injuries, your daughter can never have sex or a baby. The criminal is arrested and tried in court. To your dismay, however, the judge sets the rapist free on the grounds that we cannot precisely calculate the amount of your daughter's unhappiness. You would think that the judge's decision is deplorable and that the rapist should suffer as much as your daughter.

Which punishment is more appropriate for the rapist, two years in prison or twenty years? You would think that the latter is more appropriate than the former. When you think so, however, you are operating under the assumption that we can *roughly* calculate the amount of unhappiness. As long as we can roughly calculate the amount of unhappiness, we do not have to give up the judicial principle that the perpetrator should suffer as much as the victim. By the parity of reasoning, we do not have to give up utilitarianism insofar as we can roughly measure the amount of happiness.

4. Kant

4.1. The First Formulation

Let me begin with an everyday example. Imagine that you litter in a park. Obviously, you violated the rule, "Don't litter." Suppose, however, that when you did it, you thought that everyone else should abide by the rule and that you were an exception to the rule. Thus, you treated yourself kindly and others unkindly. In such a case, Immanuel Kant (1724-1804) would say that your act of littering in the park was immoral.

Imagine again that you were tempted to litter. However, you suppressed the urge and did not litter. You followed the rule "Don't litter in a park" because you thought that everyone including yourself should follow the rule. Kant would say that your act of not littering in the park was moral.

Suppose, for another example, that you had a few beers with your friends, got drunk and then drove home. You broke the rule "Don't drive drunk." Suppose that when you did it, you thought that everyone should comply with the rule. You thought that if everyone breaks the rule, you might be injured by a drunk driver on the road. In such a case, Kant would say that your act of driving drunk was wrong. You believed that you were an exception to the rule, treating yourself leniently and others harshly for your selfish reason.

Suppose now that you had some beers with your friends. You wanted to drive yourself home, but you did not. You acted on the rule "Don't drive drunk" because you thought that everyone, including yourself, should observe the rule. Kant would say that your act was moral. You treated yourself and others equally, not absolving yourself from the obligation that you expected of others.

A maxim is a rule related to morality. Some examples are "Keep a promise," "Kill others for fun," "Tell the truth," and "Tell a lie when that makes everyone happy." The action of keeping the promise falls under the maxim "Keep a promise," the action of killing others for fun falls under the maxim "Kill others for fun," the action of telling the truth falls under the maxim "Tell the truth," and the action of telling a lie when you have to falls under the maxim "Tell a lie when that makes everyone happy."

A universal law is a maxim that everyone follows. The maxim "Keep a promise" is not a universal law because some people break their promises. The maxim "Don't kill others" is not a universal law either because some people kill other people. The maxim "Love your child" is a universal law either because some parents do not love their parents. A question arises as to whether a universal law exists or not.

A universal law is different in kind from criminal and civil laws, which are enacted by governments for their citizens. A universal law is also different in kind from the laws of gravity, the law of conservation of mass-energy, and other laws of nature discovered by scientists. In my view, the term 'universal law' is misleading. If I were Kant, I would use the term 'universal maxim' instead of 'universal law.'

We are now ready to tackle the categorical imperative: *"act only according to that maxim through which you can at the same time will that it should become a universal law"* (Kant, 1785/2011: 71). What this sentence means is that your action is moral if and only if you will your maxim to become a universal law, i.e., if and only if you want everyone to follow your maxim. Your action is immoral if and only if you do not will your maxim to become a universal law, i.e., you do not want everyone to abide by your maxim.

According to Kantianism, in order to determine whether your action is moral or immoral, you should first formulate a maxim under which your action falls, and then ask yourself whether you will your maxim to become a universal law or not, i.e., whether you want everyone to follow it or not. If you will your maxim to become a universal law, your action is moral. If you do not, your action is immoral. Let me present some examples.

Suppose that you are about to commit murder. The first step to determine whether your action would be moral or immoral is to formulate a relevant maxim. The relevant maxim in this case is "Kill others." Secondly, you should ask yourself "Do I will my maxim to become a universal law?" If your answer is yes, your commission of murder is moral. If your answer no, your commission of murder is immoral.

Suppose, for another example, that you are contemplating driving drunk. The way to determine whether your driving drunk is right or wrong is first to formulate a maxim under which driving drunk falls. The relevant maxim in this case is "Drive drunk." Next, you should ask yourself "Do I will my maxim to become a universal law?" i.e., "Do I want everyone to drive drunk?" If your answer to this question is yes, your action of driving drunk is moral. If it is no, your action of driving drunk is immoral.

Suppose, to take another example, that you are contemplating smoking in the subway train. The way to determine whether your smoking in the subway train is right or wrong is first to formulate a maxim under which your action falls. The relevant maxim in this case is "Smoke in the subway train." Next, you should ask yourself "Do I will my maxim to become a universal law?" i.e., "Do I want everyone to smoke in the subway train?" If your answer to this question is yes, your action of smoking in the subway train is moral. If it is no, your action of smoking in the subway train is immoral.

According to Kantianism, it does not matter whether your action maximizes happiness or unhappiness. Your action might be moral even if it causes unhappiness to others. For example, as long as you will the maxim "Smoke in the subway train" to become a universal law, your action of smoking in the subway train is moral, although it maximizes unhappiness.

In addition, it does not matter whether *other people* will your maxim to become a universal law or not. As long as *you* will your maxim to become a universal law, your action is moral. Imagine that you are a smoker and other people in the subway train are nonsmokers, so you will your maxim "Smoke in the subway train" to become a universal law, but the other people do not. Even so, your action of smoking in the subway train is moral. You do not have to ask other people whether they agree with your maxim or not, and you do not have to care what maxims other people will to become universal laws. As long as *you* will your maxim to become a universal law, whatever you do is moral.

Kantianism comes down to the suggestion that you ought to treat yourself and others equally. You should not treat yourself as an exception to your own rule. An immoral act arises when you think that others should follow a rule, but you do not have to. In that sense, Kantianism is similar to the Golden Rule: Do unto others as you would have them do onto you, i.e., treat others as you want to be treated. The Gold Rule claims that you should treat yourself and others equally and that it is wrong to be kind to yourself and unkind to others.

It is a mistake to ascribe to Kant the naïve view that an act is moral when everyone accepts it. On this misguided view, it is moral to save a drowning child because everyone commends it, and murder is immoral because everyone condemns it. This view is far from Kantianism. For Kant, an act can be moral even if everyone disapproves of it. Suppose, for example, that other people disagree with driving drunk. Even so, your drinking drunk is moral as long as you will the maxim "Drive drunk" to become a universal law. Thus, when we determine whether an act is moral or immoral, we do not need to take into account whether everyone accepts it or rejects it. Insofar as *you* will *your* maxim to become a universal law, whatever you do is moral.

Let me contrast Kantian way with the utilitarian way to morally evaluate a human conduct. Recall that for utilitarians, an act is moral when it maximizes happiness, and is immoral when it maximizes unhappiness. For Kant, however, the maximization of happiness or unhappiness is an irrelevant factor. So it does not figure into the Kantian appraisal of a human conduct. We only need to check whether or not an agent wills his maxim to become a universal law or not. Utilitarians and Kantians have different strategies for determining whether an act is right or wrong because they have different views about what makes an action right or wrong. For utilitarians, the maximization of happiness is what makes an act moral. For Kantians, an agent's will that his maxim should become a universal law is what makes an act moral.

Is Kantianism tenable? Richard Hare (1970) presents a counterexample. He asks us to imagine that a Nazi wills the maxim "Kill Jews" to become a universal law and that he acts on that maxim himself. He does not mind others acting on the maxim because he knows that he is not a Jew. Since he is not a Jew, he is only pleased to kill Jews and to watch others kill Jews. According to Kantianism, the Nazi's genocidal act is right. Intuitively, however, his genocidal act is immoral. Therefore, Kantianism is false.

Let me offer a different counterexample. Consider that Mother Teresa was an altruistic person. She lived a painful life to take care of the underprivileged. Intuitively, her altruism is moral. Kantianism, however, has an absurd consequence that her altruism is immoral. Mother Teresa's sacrificial act falls under the maxim "Live an altruistic life." Suppose, however, that Mother Teresa believed that other people should not live an altruistic life because such a life is painful. This means that she did not will the maxim "Live an altruistic life" to become a universal law. She was kind to others, but not to herself. She did not treat herself and others equally. Consequently, her act was immoral according to Kantianism. Therefore, Kantianism is false.

A moral act might violate the categorical imperative. Killing others in self-defense is moral. But it violates the categorical imperative insofar as you do not want others to act on the maxim "Kill others in self-defense." You do not want others to act on that maxim because you do not want to be killed when you attack them. So your self-defense violates the categorical imperative. Yet, your behavior is moral. So moral behavior may violate the categorical imperative. It is not the case, contra Kant, that to be moral is to comply with the categorical imperative.

Immoral behavior might conform to the categorical imperative. Suicide bombers blow themselves up along with many innocent people. Their action is immoral. But it complies with the categorical imperative because they want others to act on the maxim "Kill yourself along with others!" They will that maxim to become a universal law because they are resolved to die. Therefore, conforming to the categorical imperative does not guarantee morality.

Finally, two people might will contradictory maxims to become universal laws. The poor want everyone to follow the maxim "Help the poor!" But the rich want everyone to follow the maxim "Don't help the poor." So the poor's action of helping the poor is moral, but so is the rich's not helping the poor. But how can the action of helping the poor and the action of not helping the poor both be moral? Kant owes us an answer to this question.

4.2. The Second Formulation

The second formulation of the categorical imperative states that you always treat humanity "in your own person as well as in the person of any other, always at the same time as an end, never merely as a means" (Kant, 1785/2011: 87). On this account, then, morality consists in treating people as an end, and immorality in treating them merely as a means. But what does it mean to say that we treat people as ends and as means? I treat others as ends and as means, respectively, when I act and do not act on a maxim that I think they would find acceptable. Let me present several examples to explicate this difficult notion.

Suppose that I enter a barbershop to get a haircut. I believe that the barber would find the maxim "Get a haircut at a designated fee" acceptable. So I act on that maxim, i.e., I get a haircut and pay the designated price. When I do so, I treat the barber as an end. By contrast, suppose that I get a haircut but that I do not pay the fee, even if I believe that the barber would find the maxim "Get a haircut for free" unacceptable. When I do so, I treat the barber merely as a means.

Suppose that I believe that others would find the maxim "Save a drowning child" acceptable. So I act on that maxim, i.e., I save a drowning child. I respect what I take to be the child's wish to be saved. So it is moral for me to save a drowning child.

Suppose that I do not believe that people would take the maxim "Steal from others" to be acceptable. Nevertheless, I steal from them. My action is not in accordance with the maxim that I think that others would find acceptable. I disrespect what I take to be their thoughts and wishes. Thus, my stealing is immoral.

Suppose that the US government deploys its troops to a troubled region for its own national interest. In a sense, the government uses the troops as a means for its end which is to promote the national interest. But the government is at the same time treating the troops as an end. After all, the government is acting on the maxim "Deploy the troops to a troubled region." The government believes that the maxim would be acceptable to the troops. The basis for the belief is that the troops agreed to serve in the military in the full knowledge that they could be deployed to troubled places. So the government is treating the troops both as an end and as a means.

Suppose that a girl wants to become a pianist, but her parents want her to become a judge so that they could brag about their daughter to their friends. So they tell her to prepare for LSAT despite her wish to play piano. She is punished if she disobeys. The parents are treating their child as a means for their end which is to satisfy themselves. They are not treating her as an end because to treat their daughter as an end is to act on a maxim which they think that she would find acceptable. They do not believe that the maxim "Parents should choose the career path on behalf of their child" would be acceptable to their child. Yet, they acted on that maxim. So they failed to treat her as an end.

My acting on a maxim that I think that people *would* find acceptable is different from my acting on a maxim that people *actually* find acceptable. In other words, the maxim does not have to be actually accepted by others in order for my act to be moral. Insofar as I believe that others would accept a maxim, my action in accordance with it is moral. Suppose, for example, that I am a man believing that men and women alike enjoy obscene jokes. So I act on the maxim "Tell an obscene joke" in front of women. I thought that the maxim would be acceptable to women. So I treated them as an end, hence my telling the joke is moral. Note that what I took to be their thoughts and wishes might not coincide with their actual thoughts and wishes. Even so, I acted morally. Now, suppose that the women rebuke me, saying that an obscene joke is offensive to them. I now realize that the maxim is unacceptable to the women. Despite the realization, however, I tell the women another obscene joke. My action was not in accordance with a maxim that I think that others would find agreeable. It follows that I failed to treat them as ends, hence it was immoral for me to tell them the obscene joke.

The difference between the first and the second formulations of the categorical imperative is that *my* will figures in the first formulation whereas *what I take to be their will* does in the second formulation. The first formulation dictates me to ask myself "Do I will this maxim to become a universal law?" If my answer is yes, I can act on that maxim. If it is no, I cannot. In contrast, the second formulation dictates me to ask myself "Do I think that others would will this maxim to become a universal law?" If my answer is yes, I can act on the maxim. If it is no, I cannot.

A virtue of the second formulation of the categorical imperative is, it is claimed, that it can handle counterexamples leveled against the first formulation of the categorical imperative. Recall that suicide bombers' behavior is immoral, but it conforms to the first formulation of the categorical imperative. Now, this counterexample allegedly does not refute the second formulation of the categorical imperative. Suicide bombers do not treat their victims as ends, the reason being that they do not think that their victims would find the maxim "Kill others along with yourself" acceptable. Nonetheless, they blew them up along with themselves, so their behavior is immoral.

In my view, however, the second formulation of the categorical imperative is just as problematic as the first. Suppose that suicide bombers are trying to blow themselves up along with others. Is it moral or immoral to stop them? It is clearly moral. But the second formulation of the categorical imperative implies that it is immoral. After all, you are acting on the maxim "Stop suicide bombers" when you stop them, although you believe that the suicide bombers would find the maxim unacceptable. So you are not treating them as an end.

Kant might reply that suicide bombers are acting on a bad maxim and that when people act on bad maxims, it is moral for us to stop them. A problem with this reply, however, is that it is not clear how we can distinguish between good and bad maxims. Kant might propose that a maxim is good when we act on it, we are treating others as an end, and a maxim is bad when we act on it, we are treating others merely as a means. This proposal, however, commits the fallacy of begging the question. The notions of treating others as an end and as a means were originally proposed to explicate what it is for an action to be good and bad. It is circular to explicate what it is for a maxim to be good and bad by invoking the notions of treating others as an end and as a means. That is like saying, "She can afford that nice car because she is rich, and she is rich because she can afford the nice car."

Kant might now propose that a good maxim results in the maximization of happiness and that a bad maxim results in the maximization of unhappiness. If, however, he puts forward this proposal, his ethical theory would lose its identity and collapse into utilitarianism. Utilitarians analyze the concept of morality in terms of the concept of happiness. But Kant in effect analyzed the concept of morality in terms of the concept of end. But when the concept of end is challenged, he appeals to the concept of happiness. This move amounts to explaining the concept of morality in terms of the concept of happiness, which is exactly what utilitarianism does. Thus, Kant's ethical theory would be reduced to utilitarianism.

Finally, let me present an everyday counterexample against the second formulation of the categorical imperative. Suppose that a female subordinate has sex with her male supervisor in order to get a promotion. She acts on the maxim "Offer sex to your boss in return for a promotion," thinking that her boss would find the maxim acceptable. He acts on the maxim "Accept the offer of sex in return for a promotion," thinking that his female subordinate would find the maxim acceptable. They treat each other as ends. So their behaviors comply with the second formulation of the categorical imperative. But they are wrong. So treating others as ends does not necessarily coincide with being moral, pace Kant.

5. The Veil of Ignorance

John Rawls (1971) has come up with a brilliant way to determine whether something is moral or immoral. Imagine that you are about to be born. You are allowed to choose between two worlds: World 1 and World 2. In World 1, the population is composed of 80% whites and 20% blacks. There is no racial discrimination. High offices are distributed on the basis of qualifications. In World 2, the general population is also composed of 80% whites and 20% blacks. But there is racial discrimination. Skin color is a dominant factor in the distribution of high offices.

You are behind the veil of ignorance, which means that you do not know whether you will be born black or white. Your race is determined the moment you choose a world. Once you choose a world, you cannot take the decision back, and you are thrown into the world right away. Which world would you choose? You will probably choose World 1 because you do not want to be discriminated against. On Rawls's account, racial discrimination is immoral by virtue of the fact that you would disapprove of it when you do not know about the color of your skin.

The general formulation of Rawls's theory is that something is moral just in case it would be approved of behind the veil of ignorance. To determine whether a social system is just or unjust, we only need to perform a thought experiment: Imagine that we meet as equals around a bargaining table. We are drawing up a social contract to ensure that our society is just. In this bargaining situation we are behind the veil of ignorance, i.e., we are ignorant of our race, religion, sex, natural talent, physical look, social position, national origin, and the like. To say something is moral is to say that it would be approved of in this hypothetical situation.

Rawls's account of morality is radically different from utilitarianism. Recall that according to utilitarianism, happiness is what makes something moral. But happiness does not figure in Rawls's account of morality. Rawls does not say that racism is wrong because it brings about unhappiness to blacks or because it disrupts the harmony of society. Rather, he says that it is wrong because it would be disapproved of behind the veil of ignorance, viz., it would be rejected in a hypothetical situation where we are ignorant of our race.

Rawls's theory of morality is an improvement over that of Kant (Schick and Vaughn, 2010: 404). A counterexample against Kantianism is that a Nazi, knowing that he is not a Jew, might will the maxim

"Kill all the Jews" to become a universal law. If Kantianism is true, his will makes his killing Jews moral. But our intuition says that his will does not make his action moral, so Kantianism is false. Now, if the Nazi is behind the veil of ignorance, i.e., if he does not know whether he is a Nazi or a Jew, he would not will the maxim to become a universal law. After all, he knows that he might be killed if everyone acts on it. Thus, the maxim "Kill all the Jews" would be disapproved of behind the veil of ignorance. So acting on it results in immoral acts.

6. Virtue Ethics

A happy life requires a good job, a good family, and good friends. Not everyone can have these things. Only a virtuous person can have them. A virtue is an admirable quality which disposes a person to believe in truths and do right things.

For Aristotle, there are two kinds of virtues: intellectual and moral. Intellectual virtues, such as wisdom and intelligence, help us to discover truths. Moral virtues, such as temperance, generosity, and courage, help us to stay between the two extremes: excess and defect. A courageous person, for example, maintains the balance between the vices of foolhardiness and cowardice. With respect to money, there are three kinds of people: stingy, extravagant, and generous. Stingy people spend too little. Extravagant people spend too much. Generous people spend properly. Stingy and extravagant people are shunned by others. Only generous people are liked by others, and live a happy life.

An intellectual virtue can be acquired in the classroom. A moral virtue, in contrast, can only be acquired through deeds. So we have to habitually perform virtuous acts in order to be virtuous and live a happy life. It is not enough to understand what acts are good.

In virtue ethics, the primary unit of moral evaluation is not an action but a person. According to Aristotle, a bad person is one who deviates from the golden mean to an extreme. For example, a shoplifter deviates from the middle ground of self-control to the extreme of avarice. Such a person cannot live a happy life.

According to virtue ethics, a moral act is one that a virtuous person would do. So in order to determine whether an act is right or wrong, we have to think about whether a virtuous person would approve of it or not. Recall that a virtuous person stays in the middle between excess and defect. If such a person would do something, it is moral. If not, immoral.

It is not clear, however, that such a thought experiment is helpful in resolving a controversial moral dispute. Consider the dispute between people who are pro-choice and those who are pro-life. Which side would a virtuous person support? Who deviated from the golden mean, abortionists or antiabortionists? It might be that they are both in the golden mean. Or it might be that they are in each extreme, and skeptics are in the golden mean. Thus, we have no idea whether the golden mean points to pro-choice or pro-life. Virtue ethics does not yield any means to resolve a practical moral dispute.

7. Applications

7.1. The Death Penalty

Is the death penalty right or wrong? Should it be maintained or abolished? An answer to this question can be sought from the applications of the ethical theories depicted in the previous sections. We will explore what each ethical theory has to say about this issue in this section. It will be clear that all of them produce different methods to determine whether capital punishment is right or wrong and that none of them will settle the dispute. But they will bring our discussion to a higher level.

Recall that according to the divine command theory, God's will determines whether an act is moral or immoral. Specifically, if God commands it, it is right; if God prohibits it, it is wrong. So we only need to know about God's will to resolve the dispute as to whether the death penalty is right or wrong. The best place to discover God's will is the Bible. The Bible states that "He that curseth his father or his mother, shall surely be put to death" (Exod. 21: 17). So the death penalty is allowed in the Bible, and Christianity is compatible with the death penalty.

Some theists might retort that Christianity rejects the death penalty. The passage from the Bible is used figuratively, and it should not be interpreted literally. Capital punishment is cruel, but God is merciful, so he would not command it.

This reply, however, opens a Pandora's Box. Critics might object that other sentences in the Bible are used figuratively. The Bible says, for example, that God created the universe. But that is just a metaphor. In reality, God did not create the universe. The Bible also says that God loves human beings. But that is just another metaphor. In reality, God does not love human beings.

In order to meet this objection, theists have to come up with a principled criterion for interpreting the Bible literally and non-literally, which is a formidable task, to say the least. In any case, that is how the dialectic for and against the death penalty would go within the framework of the divine command theory.

Let's now turn to cultural relativism. Recall that cultural relativism holds that a culture determines whether an act is moral or immoral. So if Korean culture says yes to the death penalty, it is right in Korea. If American culture says no to it, it is wrong in the US. An opinion poll is the best way to find out the will of a culture, so we are to follow the result of an opinion poll. Any attempt to engage in discussions or to persuade others with evidence is just a waste of time. An accurate opinion poll is all we need to discover whether capital punishment is right or wrong.

What the UN does goes against what cultural relativism says about the death penalty. The UN encourages countries around the world to abolish the death penalty on the grounds that it violates human rights. If cultural relativism is true, the UN should stop interfering with the cultural practice of countries around the world.

Let's now move on to utilitarianism. Recall that utilitarianism asserts that an act is moral when it maximizes happiness; it is immoral when it maximizes unhappiness. So in order to determine whether the death penalty is moral or immoral, we only need to calculate the amount of happiness and the amount of unhappiness it brings about. If the amount of happiness outweighs the amount of unhappiness, it is moral. If the amount of unhappiness outweighs the amount of happiness, it is immoral. So the utilitarians supporting the death penalty would argue that capital punishment deters potential criminals from committing capital crimes. As a result, the society is better off, so it must be retained. The utilitarians opposing the death penalty would counter that there is no decisive evidence that the death penalty deters murder more than life imprisonment and that it only increases unhappiness of the condemned and their families. This is how pros and cons of the death penalty would argue for their positions within the framework of utilitarianism.

Utilitarianism, however, cannot resolve the dispute over the death penalty for two reasons. First, it is difficult to tell which weighs more, the amount of happiness or the amount of unhappiness that the death penalty generates. Second, even if the amount of happiness outweighs the amount of unhappiness, some might argue that we should bring justice to capital offenders.

Let's apply Kantianism to the issue of the death penalty. Recall that according to Kantianism, my action is moral when I will my maxim to become a universal law. So the issue boils down to whether I will the maxim "Execute a capital offender" to become a universal law or not. If I will the maxim to become a universal law, it is moral for me to execute a capital offender. If I do not, it is immoral for me to do so.

A problem with this strategy to resolve the dispute over the death penalty is that some people might will the maxim "Execute a capital offender" to become a universal law, while other people might not. So Kantianism does not yield a solution to the issue of the death penalty.

What would Rawls say? Recall that according to him, what makes something right is that it would be approved of behind the veil of ignorance. To determine whether capital punishment is moral or immoral, we only need to perform a thought experiment: Imagine that we meet as equals around a bargaining table to draw up an ideal social contract. Our goal is to live in a fair society. We are behind the veil of ignorance, so we do not know whether we would be capital offenders, murder victims, capital offenders' family members, or victims' family members. Capital punishment is moral as long as it would be approved of in this hypothetical situation.

A problem with this strategy to resolve the dispute over the death penalty is that some contractors might approve of the death penalty, while others might not. Some might even abstain from making a decision. So Rawls's theory does not yield a solution to the issue of the death penalty.

Can Aristotle's virtue ethics be used to resolve the dispute over the death penalty? If a virtuous person, a person who stays in the golden mean, supports the death penalty, the death penalty should be retained. But it is not clear, however, whether a virtuous person would support or oppose the death penalty. Therefore, virtue ethics does not yield guidance as to whether the death penalty is moral or immoral.

7.2. Suicide

Suicide is a prevalent phenomenon in the world. Nearly everyone contemplates suicide at least once. Is suicide moral or immoral? Aquinas, a medieval philosopher, argued that under no circumstance is suicide moral. He put forward three interesting arguments to justify his position. We will go over them in this section. In addition, we will examine two popular arguments in defense of suicide.

Let me begin with Aquinas's first argument against suicide. He invokes the notion of natural inclination in his first argument against suicide. We have the natural inclinations to eat, to sleep, to have children, and to love them. Parents love their children not because they are educated to love them but because they are genetically programmed to do so. We also have the natural inclination to love ourselves:

> First, everything naturally loves itself, and it is for this reason that everything naturally seeks to keep itself in being and to resist hostile forces. So suicide runs counter to one's natural inclinations. (Aquinas, 1975: 33)

In other words, suicide is morally wrong because it runs counter to our natural inclinations to love and preserve ourselves.

The foregoing argument can be undermined by the three considerations. First, we have the natural inclination to avoid intense and persistent pain. Under certain circumstances, death is the only way to terminate such pain. To use Fred Feldman's example (1992: 210), a cancer patient might be in such pain, and there might be no chance at all that he will recover. It is not clear that suicide is impermissible even in such circumstances. If Aquinas thinks otherwise, he faces a difficult question: What is the point of enduring the horrible pain until the patient dies?

Second, imagine that a psychopath kills many people and that the police close in around him. He is afraid of being sent to prison and to death row. He would rather die before that happens. He kills himself before being arrested and before he kills anyone else. He went against his natural inclination to preserve himself. In such a case, however, suicide is legitimate. If Aquinas thinks otherwise, he owes us an account of why he thinks as he does.

Third, Jung-geun An, a Korean patriot, went against his natural inclination to preserve himself when he assassinated Ito Hirobumi, a Japanese official, in the early 20th century when Korea was a colony of Japan. The Korean patriot was arrested and executed by th e Japanese. He loved himself, but his love for his country outweighed his love for himself. He knew that he would die if he killed the Japanese official. So in a sense he committed suicide. Most Koreans, however, do not condemn him. They revere him as a national hero.

Let me turn to Aquinas's second argument against suicide. If you take your own life, that saddens your family members and friends left behind:

> Second, every part belongs to the whole in virtue of what it is. But every man is part of the community, so that he belongs to the community in virtue of what he is. Suicide therefore involves damaging the community. (Aquinas, 1975: 33)

To put it differently, suicide is wrong because it has a negative consequence on the community. It seems agreeable that suicide makes some people unhappy in *most* cases.

It is disagreeable, however, that suicide *always* makes some people unhappy. Suppose, to use Feldman's example again, that the cancer patient has neither family members nor friends. He does not damage the community when he kills himself. On the contrary, he might save the government from the cost of his medical treatment. Similarly, the psychopath's suicide does not have a negative impact on the community. If anything, the community is better off if he dies by suicide because other lives will be saved and the government would not have to spend tax money on a trial. These examples indicate that suicide does not damage the community in *some* cases, although it does in *most* cases. Thus, it was wrong for Aquinas to say that suicide is always deplorable.

Let me turn to Aquinas's third argument against suicide. He was a theologian believing that God exists. It is not surprising that his third argument against suicide relies on the religious notion that suicide amounts to a challenge to God's authority:

> Third, life is a gift made to man by God. It is subject to him who is *master of death and life*. Therefore, a person who takes his own life sins against God. ⋯ God alone has authority to decide about life and death. (Aquinas, 1975: 33)

In short, suicide is bad because God would disapprove of it. This argument should be convincing to religious believers.

But what about atheists and agnostics? Atheists do not believe that God exists; Agnostics are not sure. The third argument would not be convincing to them. In order for the argument to be persuasive, it has to be proven first that God exists. That, however, is a daunting task, as we have seen in the previous chapter.

Let me say, however, that the foregoing criticism against the third argument is cheap. Anybody can raise such an objection. An intelligent person would criticize the third argument under the assumption that God exists.

Let's assume for the sake of argument that God exists. Even so, perverse questions arise. What if the gift from God, viz., life, is bad? Why should we put up with it? What is wrong with returning it to him and asking for a better one? It is not clear how Aquinas could answer these questions. Moreover, given that God is all-good, he should have given me a good gift. But he gave me a bad gift. It is not clear why he gave me the bad gift while he gave other people good ones.

Moreover, it is debatable that God alone has authority to decide life and death. Under certain circumstances, a human being has such authority. Imagine that a robber breaks into my house and tries to kill me and my family. So I kill him before he kills me. I made a decision about his life to defend myself and my family members. My action is performed in self-defense, and it is legitimate. We can imagine other situations where it is justifiable for humans to kill each other. I leave this task to readers.

Let me turn to two popular arguments for suicide. First, consider that I have a computer. It is my property, so if I want to destroy it, I can. By the same token, my body is my property. So if I want to smoke or gain weight, I can. I can do those, even if doing them harms my health and shortens my life span. To go further, I can put an end to my own life. This line of reasoning can be summarized in the following standard form:

I own my body.
I can do whatever I want to do to my body.
∴ Suicide is permissible.

Put differently, I have the right to die at the time of my own choosing. Other people should respect my decision. They do not have the right to interfere with my decision about what I can do to my body.

This argument is problematic. Your body is not completely yours. After all, you owe yourself to your parents and to your community, given that your parents and your community have provided you with food, clothes, a house, and all sorts of other commodities. Your body is partially owned by your parents and by your community. Therefore, their consent is required before you destroy it.

Second, suppose that you borrowed a lot of money from a private moneylender, you cannot pay the money back, the moneylender presses you hard to repay the debt, and as a result you want to put an end to your suffering. The following argument occurs in your mind:

> I would be better off dead than alive.
> ∴Suicide is moral.

To put it another way, suicide is justifiable in circumstances where death is better than life. In such cases, we can welcome the Grim Reaper.

Is the preceding argument plausible? Two critical responses are possible. First, our life is vicissitudinous, i.e., there are ups and downs in our life. We may be miserable now, but we may be happy in the future. Only people who endured and survived trials and tribulations deserve successful and happy lives. As the saying goes, there is the bright sun behind the dark clouds.

Second, you can say that an apple is more delicious than an orange, only if you have tasted both an apple and an orange before. If you have never tasted an apple before, you cannot say that an apple is tastier than an orange. Analogously, if you have never experienced death, you cannot say that death is better than life. Given that you do not know what it is like to be dead, you can never be justified in believing that you would be better off dead than alive.

8. Why Should We Be Moral?

Why should we be moral? Why should we do right things and refrain from doing wrong things? This section aims to answer this question.

Suppose that a rich man lives alone next door to me that he is out of town on vacation. He is known to keep one million dollars in his apartment, and I have a master key. It looks like I can steal his money and get away with it. But should I? If not, why not? There can be two different answers to this question. One might be called the religious view, and the other the secular view.

According to the religious view, I should not steal the money from the rich man because if I do, I will be punished by God after I die. If I refrain from stealing the money, I will be rewarded by God after I die. To generalize, if we live a moral life, we will enjoy the eternal bliss from God after we die. If we live an immoral life, we will suffer from the eternal damnation from God after we die. Therefore, we should do right things and refrain from doing wrong things.

According to the secular view, we should be moral because if we are moral, we will be rewarded by our fellow human beings while we are alive. If we are immoral, we will be punished by our fellow human beings while we are alive. Thus, if we want to live a happy life, we should be moral. For example, I should not break into the rich man's apartment because there is a possibility that I might be caught. He might come back home earlier than scheduled, or his family member might drop by to see how he is doing. Since I cannot rule out such possibilities, I should not break into his apartment.

What if I can rule out such possibilities? In other words, I know that the rich man will definitely not come back home earlier than scheduled and that he does not have anyone stopping by his apartment. Even in such a situation, I should not steal the money from him. Why not? I might feel remorseful. Guilt should not be underestimated. For some people, the guilt feeling is intense and long lasting. After suffering from bad dreams for several years, they confess to their victims and seek to be forgiven, or they turn themselves in to the police and go to jail. The guilt we suffer might outweigh the benefit we derive from the rich man's money.

What if I am remorseless? Even so, it is still in my interest not to steal the money from my neighbor. If I steal the money from him, I will have a lot of fun with the money. After I spend all the money, however, I will feel the temptation to steal money from others again.

When the temptation arises, I should either suppress it or yield to it. Suppressing it is painful, requiring patience and self-denial because I cannot easily shake off the sweet memory that I acquired with the money. So I yield to the temptation and steal money again. Again, I use up the money, feel the temptation, and yield to it. I become a slave of the temptation and form the habit of stealing money from others. A problem with the habit is that it seldom goes unnoticed. If I do wrong things again and again, I will eventually be caught. Thus, I should not take the first wrong step. It is short-sighted to see the close pleasure, but not the big pain behind it.

A problem with the secular view is, as Stephen Layman says, the "lives of relatively good people are often miserable, while the wicked prosper" (1991: 27). Thus, we should live a moral life not because if we live a moral life, we will be happy in this world but because if we live a moral life, we will be rewarded by God after we die. So claims Layman.

Layman's criticism of the secular view is convincing. But we do not have to give up the secular view entirely. It can be modified as follows. If we are moral, we are *likely* to live a happy life; if we are immoral, we are *likely* to live an unhappy life. This modest version of the secular view is compatible with the existence some moral people living an unhappy life and with the existence of some immoral people living a happy life.

Suppose that three swimmers spot a child drowning in a lake

(Schick and Vaughn, 2010: 362-363). The first swimmer does not feel like saving the child. But someone on a wheelchair points a shotgun at him, and says, "If you don't save the child, I'll blow your head off." He reluctantly jumps into the water and saves the child. In contrast, the second swimmer voluntarily jumps into the water and saves the child. He does so in the hope that he will receive a reward from the child's parents. The third swimmer voluntarily jumps into the water and saves the child. He does so, however, thinking that it is the right thing to do. He feels pleasure in saving the child.

All the three swimmers do the right thing, but for different reasons. The first one does it for fear of punishment. The second one does it to be rewarded. The third one does it for the sake of itself. Which person is the most morally praiseworthy? Of course, the third one is. Thus, a morally good person lives a moral life for the sake of the moral life, not for the sake of avoiding punishment or for the sake of receiving a reward from God (Schick and Vaughn, 2010: 362-363).

I must point out, though, that theists might perform good deeds out of the desire to do good as well as out of the desire to avoid punishment from God and out of the desire to be rewarded from God. In other words, the three desires to do right things are not mutually exclusive.

Study Questions

1. State and criticize the divine command theory and cultural relativism.

2. State and criticize utilitarianism and Kantianism. Focus on the first formulation of the categorical imperative when you discuss Kantianism.

3. Of the divine command theory, cultural relativism, utilitarianism, Kantianism, and Rawls's theory, which one yields the best method to determine whether the death penalty is right or wrong? Why?

4. Is it moral to euthanize people who are terminally ill? Was it right for President Truman to drop atomic bombs on Japan to end the Second World War? Is same-sex marriage justifiable? Should drugs be legalized? Is cloning a human permissible? Choose at least one of these questions and answer it from the utilitarian perspective.

5. Is it moral to euthanize people who are terminally ill? Was it right for President Truman to drop atomic bombs on Japan to end the Second World War? Is same-sex marriage justifiable? Should drugs be legalized? Is cloning a human permissible? Choose at least one of these questions and answer it from the Kantian perspective.

6. Should we retain or abolish the death penalty? Apply the divine command theory, cultural relativism, utilitarianism, Kantianism, and Rawls's view to the issue.

7. State and evaluate one of Aquinas's three arguments for the immorality of suicide. (To evaluate an argument means to determine whether the argument is good or bad. You can do this by giving your own reasons for agreeing or disagreeing with the argument.)

8. Defend or criticize the two popular arguments for suicide. Alternatively, make your own case for or against the permissibility of suicide.

9. Why should we live a moral life? What are the weaknesses and strengths of the religious view and the secular view? Which view do you prefer? Why?

CHAPTER

04

Philosophy of Mind

What is the mind? How does it differ from the matter? How is it related to the body? Can the mind control the body? If not, why not? These are the questions that this chapter attempts to answer.

1. "I think, therefore I am."

Can we know about the world? If so, what is the source of knowledge? An initial answer to this question is that knowledge comes from experience. We know about the world because we observe it. For example, I know that there is a book on the table because I see it with my eyes. It looks like we know about the world through sense-experience. René Descartes (1596-1650), however, claims that sense-perception is not a reliable source of knowledge.

In order to understand what Descartes has in mind, we first need to be clear about the relationship between perception and the world. Suppose I see a book on the table. When I see it, I have a visual perception. A causal relation holds between the book and my visual perception. The book causes the visual perception. After all, photons are emitted from the book. Some of them hit my retina, creating a neural impulse. The neural impulse is transmitted via optic nerves to my brain. Finally, the visual perception occurs in my mind. This causal chain would not occur, if the book were not on the table. So it is natural to suggest that the world causes perceptions in our mind.

Descartes, however, entertains the possibility that there is an evil demon instead of the world. It is not the world but the evil demon that causes the perceptions in my mind. The evil demon is so powerful that it can create experiences that are identical to those that would be created by the world. I have the visual perception of the book, but the perception is not produced by the book. It is rather infused into my mind by the evil demon. There is nothing outside of my mind except the evil demon. There is no book, no tree, no mountain, and no world. Even my body does not exist. It appears that I have hands, but it is not my hands but the even demon which causes the perception of my hands in my mind. It follows that all of my beliefs about physical objects are false. My belief that I have hands is false because I do not have hands. My belief that there is a book on the table is likewise false. The evil demon has thoroughly deceived me about the world. All perceptions are misleading, and result in false beliefs.

Here comes Descartes's challenge. Can we prove that the evil demon does not exist? That is, can we rule out the possibility that the evil demon exists instead of the world? It seems that the answer is no. We cannot tell whether our perceptions are caused by the world or by the evil demon. So we do not know whether the world exists or not. I seem to see a book on the table. But I do not know that there is a book on the table. I seem to see my hands. But I do not know that I have hands. Skepticism is on the offing. Skepticism in this context is the view that we cannot know anything about the world. A view more radical than skepticism is solipsism, according to which the physical universe does not exist; only my mind exists. Skepticism and solipsism fly in the face of common sense, i.e., it is difficult for laypeople to accept them. It is not clear, however, what evidence we could adduce to prove that they are false.

Descartes's intention with the evil demon story is not to promote skepticism or solipsism but to show that our belief about a physical object is dubitable and fallible. That is, we can doubt that our belief about a physical object is true, and our belief about a physical object might be false. Given that we cannot rule out the possibility that the evil demon exists instead of the world, we can doubt that there is a book on the table, and our belief that there is a book on the table might be false, even though we seem to see a book on the table. Thus, sense-perception is not a reliable source of knowledge about the world. Knowledge does not come from experience.

Is there anything whose existence I cannot doubt? It is my mind. If my mind does not exist, there would be nothing for the evil demon to implant perceptions on, and nothing for the evil demon to play tricks on. In addition, if my mind does not exist, I could not even entertain the possibility that there is the evil demon instead of the physical universe. In short, the existence of my mind is a precondition for my act of doubting. The fact that I doubt that the world exists shows that I have a mind. Thus, I cannot doubt that my mind exists although I can doubt that a physical object exists.

It is also indubitable that I am in a certain mental state. Suppose that I cut my finger. As a result, I feel pain. My belief that my finger is cut is dubitable and fallible. After all, I might not even have a body. But my belief that I feel pain is indubitable and infallible. It is true that I feel pain whether the evil demon exists or the world exists. I can be certain that I feel pain, although I cannot be certain that my injured finger causes it. I cannot be wrong about my pain, although I can be wrong about my finger. In short, my belief about a physical object is dubitable and fallible, whereas my belief about my own mental state is indubitable and infallible.

Here is another example. Suppose that my stomach is empty and that consequently I feel hunger. My belief that I feel hunger is different from my belief that my stomach is empty. The former is a belief about my mind, whereas the latter is a belief about a physical object. I can doubt that my stomach is empty. After all, I might not even have a body, and there might be the evil demon instead of the physical universe. But I cannot doubt that I feel hunger. It does not matter whether the hunger is caused by the evil demon or by the empty stomach. I can be certain that my hunger exists. So my belief that I feel hunger is indubitable and infallible, but my belief that my stomach is empty is dubitable and fallible.

It is in this context that Descartes puts forward his famous motto: "I think, therefore I am." Empiricists would say, "I see my body, therefore I am." After all, for empiricists, all knowledge about the world comes from experience. But Descartes is not an empiricist but a rationalist. He believes that some knowledge about the world comes from reason, the mental capacity to think as opposed to observe. The evil demon story shows that we can doubt the existence of our body. So it is problematic to say, "I see my body, therefore I exist." But we cannot doubt that we are thinking. Thinking is a mental act whose occurrence I can be certain about even if it is caused by the evil demon. Furthermore, doubting is impossible without thinking. There is a contradiction in saying, "I doubt, but I don't think," but there is no contradiction in saying, "I doubt, but I don't have a body."

2. Descartes's Three Distinctions

How does the mind differ from the matter? An answer to this question can be extracted from Descartes's evil demon story sketched in the previous section. Recall that my belief about my mind is indubitable and infallible, but my belief about a physical object is dubitable and fallible. So my mind is something whose existence I cannot doubt, and about which I cannot have a false belief. But the matter is something whose existence I can doubt, and about which I can have a false belief. In other words, my mind is something that I can be certain about, but the matter is something that I cannot be certain about. I have a special and privileged access to my own mind, but not to a physical object. In this sense, the mind is transparent, whereas the matter is opaque.

There are problems with this distinction between the mind and the body. It is not clear that we are indeed infallible about our own mental states. Mentally ill patients might believe that their minds work properly. Their beliefs about their own minds are false. Or people whose legs are cut off might believe that they feel pain in their legs. Such a pain is called phantom pain. Their beliefs about their own mental states are false.

A more sophisticated objection goes as follows: A belief, mental or physical, is a result of our similarity judgment. I believe, for instance, that an object in front of me is an apple because I made a judgment that the present apple is similar to other apples that I encountered before. I made the judgment that the present object and the past objects belong to the same kind. Without this similarity judgment, I cannot form the belief that the present object is an apple. We are doing the same when we form a belief about our mental state. I believe, for instance, that I feel pain because I made a judgment that this mental state is similar to other mental states that I had before. I made the judgment that the present mental state and the past mental state are of the same kind. So what? Our judgment is fallible because our memory is fallible. We sometimes remember the past incorrectly. So we might form a false belief about our own mental state; we are fallible about our own mental state. So my mind is also opaque to me, just as a physical object is opaque to me.

It might be retorted, however, that although we are fallible about our own mind, it is still true that our own mind is better known to us than a physical object is (Goldman, 1993). That is, my belief about my mind is less likely to be false than my belief about a physical object.

Descartes makes another distinction between the mind and the body. The matter is extended, but the mind is not, i.e., the matter takes up space, but the mind does not. For example, the brain, a physical thing, has a spatial location, shape, size, and mass. It can be measured and weighed; the mind cannot. But the mind has none of these physical properties. We have no idea how we can go about measuring its length or weight. It might be objected that it is merely an assumption that the mind does not take up space. That is, the assumption needs to be justified. The objection is fair enough. Descartes does not provide a justification for the assumption. It must be admitted, however, that no one has yet measured and weighed the mind. That is, no one has yet given a quantitative, not qualitative, description of the mind. In the absence of such a description, we have reason to doubt that the mind is extended.

The mind is a peculiar object. It does not seem to occupy space, as Descartes points out, but it does seem to occupy time. It makes sense to say that my mind exists *now*, although it does not seem to make sense to say that my mind is *here*. In this sense, it is not like a mathematical object. A mathematical object is not in time and space. But the mind is in time, but not in space.

The final distinction between the mind and the matter that Descartes makes is that the mind is not divisible, but the matter is. A physical object can be divided into pieces, but our mind cannot be in the way an apple can be. This distinction is parasitic on the second distinction between the mind and the matter. Given that the mind does not occupy space, it cannot be divided. It is hard to imagine a divisible thing that does not exist in space. One might claim that the mind can indeed be divided. Some people suffer from dissociative identity disorder. One day they act like three-year-olds, and another day like adults. The different selves do not communicate with each other. It looks as though different minds exist in the same body. Descartes might reply, however, that given that the mind does not occupy space, it cannot be divided.

3. Interactionism

Descartes advocates interactionism, the view that the mind and the body causally affect each other. For example, my arm moves because I want to move it. I shed tears because I feel sad. The body also causally affects the mind. For example, I feel pain in my hand because my finger is cut. I feel hunger because my stomach is empty. Interactionism is intuitively appealing. It goes well with our commonsense view of the mind-body relation. We are all interactionists until we are informed of science and philosophy.

What is the reason for rejecting interactionism? Elizabeth of Bohemia (1643/1994) puts forward the following argument:

> A material object at rest moves only on contact with another material object.
> The mind cannot be in contact with the body.
> ∴The mind cannot move the body.

The first premise seems to be true. A billiard ball, for instance, moves because another billiard ball bumps into it. It would remain at rest if another body does not collide with it. The second premise also seems to be true. As Descartes claims, the mind is not extended, so it cannot be in contact with a physical object.

How does Descartes respond to Princess Elizabeth's challenge? He rejects the second premise, contending that the mind interacts with the body via the pineal gland. The pineal gland is in the brain. Thus, the mind interacts with the region of the brain, and the region of the brain interacts with the rest of the body parts. So the mind interacts with the body via the pineal gland.

Descartes's response, however, is problematic. The pineal gland is a part of the brain, and hence it is a physical thing. How does the mind interact with the physical thing, the pineal gland? The original question of how the mind interacts with the body interact remains unanswered. The putative interaction between the mind and the pineal gland is just as mysterious as the putative interaction between the mind and the body, given that the pineal gland is a part of the body. Descartes has begged the question against Princess Elizabeth.

To respond to this objection, Descartes might withdraw his previous contention that the mind is not extended, and might claim instead that the mind is extended. If the mind is extended, it is not mysterious that it moves the body. There can be a scientific explanation of how a body moves another body.

There are, however, two problems here. First, if the mind is extended, questions about the mind arise. How much volume does it occupy? No one has yet measured the volume of the mind. Furthermore, it is not clear how we could go about measuring it. Second, Descartes has to give up his other claims: our mind is transparent and indivisible. If the mind is extended as the matter is, my belief about my mind is as fallible as my belief about a physical object is, and the mind is as divisible as the matter.

Is Elizabeth's first premise tenable? Is there any case in science in which a body moves another body without making contact with it? If there are such cases in science, we do not have to accept the first premise, hence the conclusion. There seem to be such examples in science. The sun can move the Earth without making contact with it.

4. Substance Dualism

Descartes is a substance dualist. A substance can exist independently of anything else. It contrasts with property. A property is a feature that a substance possesses. For instance, a book is a substance. It has the property of being rectangular. A coin is a substance. It has the property of being circular. A property cannot exist independently of a substance. The property of being rectangular cannot exist unless the book exists. The property of being circular cannot exist without the coin.

Descartes contends that the mind and the body are different substances. Thus, his view of the mind and the body is called substance dualism. To say that the mind and the body are different substances is to say that the mind and the body can exist independently of each other. The mind can exist without the body, and vice versa. It follows that the mind can survive the death of the body and that soul exists.

Substance dualism is in contrast with property dualism: The mind is a property of the brain. To say that the mind is a property of the brain is to say that the mind cannot exist independently of the brain. If the brain dies, so does the mind. So property dualism denies the existence of soul. Most contemporary philosophers of mind reject substance dualism and accept property dualism.

What is Descartes's argument for substance dualism? The mind has the three properties that the body does not so they can exist independently of each other. Descartes's argument has the following form:

> If X and Y have different properties, they can exist independently of each other.
> The mind and the body have different properties.
> ∴The mind and the body can exist independently of each other.

A book and a coin have different properties. The book is rectangular. The coin is round. The book and the coin can exist independently of each other. As this example illustrates, if two things have different properties, they can exist independently of each other.

To refute the argument, we only need to come up with a counterexample in which X and Y have different properties, and yet, X depends on Y for its existence. It is not difficult to find such a counterexample. Fire and fuel have different properties. Fire has the property of being hot. But fuel does not. Fuel has the property of being transparent. But fire does not. Yet, fire cannot exist without fuel. This counterexample shows that Descartes's argument is invalid, i.e., the conclusion does not necessarily follow from the premise. So the mind might depend on the body for its existence, although it has properties that the body does not have.

Furthermore, we have reason to doubt that the mind can exist without the body. Can we conceive of the mind existing without the body? Descartes thinks that he can. But we do not even have a slightest idea what the mind out of the body looks like. Just try to form the image of the mind existing without the body. What is its color? Is it black or red? Does it even have a color? If so, it must emit photons. But how can a thing that does not occupy space emit photons? If it is not colored, how does it look? How long is it? Substance dualism raises more questions than answers. Hence, it makes more sense to embrace property dualism than substance dualism.

5. Epiphenomenalism

Thomas Huxley (1825-1895), an eminent biologist, espouses epiphenomenalism, according to which the mind cannot causally affect the body, although the body can causally affect the mind. To use an analogy, the mind is related to the body in the way a shadow is related to an object. The shape of a tree affects the shape of the shadow of the tree, but not vice versa:

> ..the feeling we call volition is not the cause of a voluntary act, but the symbol of that state of the brain which is the immediate cause of that act. (Huxley, 1893: 244)

On Huxley's account, what controls our body is not our mind but our brain. This view runs counter to our view of the mind-body relation. We believe that our arms move because we have the will to move them. If we do not have the will, they would not move. What is more obvious than this?

However, what is obvious is not necessarily true. It was once obvious that the Earth is at rest and that celestial bodies move around it. Look at the sky. It is obvious to us that the sun, the moon, and the stars move 15 degrees an hour to the west. It is also obvious to us that an apple is red. The apple, however, is a collection of atoms, and atoms are colorless. So in reality, the apple is colorless. It only appears to be red. These examples indicate that our commonsense view of the mind-body relation might be false, although it is obvious.

Why should we accept epiphenomenalism? Consider the following argument that I call the argument from energy:

> If something does not have energy, it cannot move another thing.
> The mind does not have energy.
> ∴The mind cannot move the body.

The first premise seems to be true. If I push a desk in front of me, it moves. It would not move unless something pushes it. I can move the desk because I have energy. The second premise also seems to be true. The mind is not extended, so it does not have mass. If something does not have mass, it does not have energy according to the equations: $E=1/2mv^2$, $E=mgh$, and $E=mc^2$. Therefore, the mind does not have energy.

Some psychological experiments support epiphenomenalism. For any mental event, there is a corresponding brain event. Benjamin Libet (1985) measured the time between a mental event and its corresponding brain event. It turns out that a mental event lags 350 to 400ms behind a brain event. For example, my desire to move my arm corresponds to a neural event in the brain. Libet's finding suggests that the neural event occurs in the brain and then slightly later the desire occurs in the mind. It follows that before the desire arises in my mind, a neural impulse has traveled to the muscles in my arms. It follows that it is not the desire to move my arm but the neural firing in the brain that causes my arm to move. Again, the mind is like a shadow that does not have a causal efficacy on the body.

Epiphenomenalism is not an absurd theory of mind. It is a philosophical basis of a certain medical practice. Suppose that you have a sudden headache and are hospitalized. Doctors will test your blood, urine, and brain to find the cause of the headache. But why do they test these *physical* things when the problem lies in your *mind*? They believe that a mental state is determined by a physical state and that the headache can be cured by manipulating the chemical state of the brain. To use another example, suppose a blood vessel is blocked by a thrombus in your brain. Stroke is imminent. Can you restore the blood flow merely by *wishing* for the thrombus to dissolve? No. The mind cannot causally affect the body! Ask neurophysiologists, "Do you believe that the mind causally affects the body?" A significant number of them will say that neurophysiology does not require the assumption that the mind causally affects the body. They will add that any mental problem can be solved by fixing a physical problem. This is the epiphenomenalist attitude.

Epiphenomenalism has a disastrous consequence on morality. We believe that we are responsible for our behavior because we have free will. For example, we believe that murderers are morally at fault because they exercised their free will when they killed someone. They chose to commit murders when they were able to choose not to. We would not blame them, if they had no choice, but epiphenomenalism says that free will and moral responsibility are illusions. We appear to have free will when we do not. We just think that we are morally responsible for our behavior when we are not. If this is so, why do we punish criminals when they are not morally responsible for their bad behavior? We send them to jail not because they are morally blameworthy but because we want to protect society from them.

Epiphenomenalism is not without problems. First, it is not clear how the body causally affects the mind. After all, the body occupies space and the mind does not, as Descartes claims. How can a thing that occupies space have a causal influence on something that does not take up space? Second, epiphenomenalists would have us believe that the mind does not have any causal efficacy on the body, i.e., that the mind does not do anything at all. Then, why does it exist? Is it an accident that the mind came into being? Epiphenomenalists have to answer these questions.

6. Reduction

This section aims to clarify the concept of reduction, a powerful conceptual tool to understand various theories of mind.

What does it mean to say that X is reducible to Y? In other words, what does it mean to say that something is reducible to another thing? It means that X, upon close examination, turns out to be Y. To put it differently, X and Y appear to be different objects, but that in reality they are one and the same object. For example, Clark Kent is reducible to superman. Clark Kent and superman appear to be different objects, but in reality they are one and the same object. Clark Kent, upon close investigation, is superman. Some examples of reduction from the history of science are as follows:

List of Reductions
- An apple is reducible to a collection of atoms.
- Water is reducible to H_2O.
- Heat is reducible to the mean kinetic energy of molecules.

- Light is reducible to the electromagnetic waves.

- Lightning is reducible to an electric discharge.

- A gene is reducible to a bunch of DNA molecules.

To say that X is reducible to Y does not mean that X is eliminated from the world. For example, water is reducible to H_2O. It does not follow that water is eliminated from the world. Water still exists, even if it is reducible to H_2O. What changes as a result of reduction is not the world but our beliefs about the world. We previously believed that X and Y were different objects, but we now believe that they are one and the same object.

An important consequence of the reduction of X to Y is that whatever is true of one is also true of the other, i.e., if X has a certain property, so does Y, and vice versa. This consequence should be obvious, given that X and Y are one and the same object. For example, if it is true that superman can fly, it should also be true that Clark Kent can fly. If it is true that light travels at 300,000km/s, so should it be true that electromagnetism travels at 300,000km/s. If what is true of X is not true of Y, X is not reducible to Y, i.e., they are distinct objects. For example, it is true that Bruce Wayne lives in Gotham City, but it is false that Superman lives in Gotham City, so Bruce Wayne is not reducible to superman, i.e., they are different objects.

What is the philosophical payoff of reduction? Our ontology, the list of things that we think exist, gets simpler as a result of reduction. Suppose that X and Y were on our ontology as separate items. Scientific research reveals, however, that X is reducible to Y. If that happens, X can be eliminated from our ontology. As a result, our ontology gets smaller. The pursuit of a simple ontology is in accordance with Ockham's razor.

Ockham's razor asserts that we should not multiply entities beyond necessity. In other words, we should choose a simple theory over a complex theory when they explain the same phenomena. Being simple does not necessarily mean being easy to understand. T_1 is simpler than T_2, if T_1 has fewer assumptions or fewer explanatory entities than T_2. Ockham's razor is a method that scientists invoke when scientific theories compete with each other.

Let's use the concept of reduction to understand some metaphysical views. What kinds of things are there in the world? Dualism claims that there are two kinds of things, mental and physical. Put differently, the mind, ideas, and the matter exist. For early modern philosophers, the word 'idea' is an umbrella term referring to all sorts of mental events: sensations, beliefs, anger, hope, and what have you. Idealism maintains that all that exists is mental, so the mind and ideas exist. Hume claims that ideas and the matter exist. Materialism holds that only material things exist in the world. These four metaphysical views can be schematized as follows:

	Mind	Ideas	Matter
Dualism	o	o	o
Idealism	o	o	x
Hume's View	x	o	o
Materialism	x	x	o

Dualism goes hand in hand with common sense. We believe that a physical object causes ideas in our mind. But the rest of the doctrines clash with common sense. Critics of idealism ask, "What about a physical object?" Idealists answer that it is reducible to a set of ideas. Hume's critics ask, "What about the mind?" Hume answers that it is reducible to a bundle of ideas. Critics of materialism ask "What about a mental state?" Materialists answer that it is reducible to a physical state. I explicate these claims in the following sections.

7. Berkeley's Idealism

For George Berkeley (1685-1753), all that exists is mental. How about a physical object? A physical object, as something that causes ideas in our mind, does not exist. What we take to be a physical object is nothing but a collection of ideas. Take an apple as an example. We see, touch, taste, smell, and hear it. As a result, visual, tactile, gustatory, olfactory, and auditory sensations arise in our mind. An apple is reducible to a collection of these sensations. An apple appears to be a physical object that causes these sensations. On close examination, however, it is a collection of the ideas. Thus, Berkeley's position is called idealism.

Idealism is different from solipsism. According to solipsism, only my mind exists. According to idealism, however, there are other minds as well as my own. Both solipsism and idealism fly in the face of common sense. Common sense tells us that a physical object causes ideas in our mind and that it is distinct from the ideas. But

Berkeley rejects the commonsensical view of a physical object.

Why should we accept idealism? What is the philosophical payoff of accepting it? We can overcome skepticism about the world once we subscribe to it. Recall that Descartes persuasively argued that there might be the evil demon instead of the physical universe, so we can doubt the existence of a physical object. So our belief about a physical object is dubitable and fallible. But my belief about my own mental state is indubitable and infallible. Now, if what we take to be a physical object is nothing but a collection of ideas as Berkeley would have us believe, our belief about the physical object is also indubitable and infallible. Thus, we can know about a physical object.

But there is a problem with idealism. What if no one perceives an apple, for instance? Does it exist or not exist? An idea is ontologically dependent upon the mind, i.e., an idea cannot exist without the mind. So if no one perceives an apple, it cannot exist. How does Berkeley reply to this objection? He replies that the apple exists because God perceives it. Idealism becomes dubious the moment Berkeley invokes God. Why not say that the apple exists, even if no one perceives it, because it is a physical object and a physical object is not reducible to a collection of ideas? Why not invoke the physical universe instead of God?

8. Hume's Bundle Theory of Mind

What is the relationship between the mind and an idea? A commonsensical answer is that an idea occurs in the mind, so the mind is an arena in which an idea comes and goes. Note that this view is wedded to the assumption that the mind is distinct from an idea. For Hume, however, the mind is reducible to a collection of ideas. There is no such thing as the mind over and above ideas. What we take to be the mind is nothing but a bundle of ideas. So his view of the mind is called the bundle theory of mind. Hume presents two arguments for this provocative theory of the mind.

The first argument is that there is not an impression of the mind, so we cannot say that the mind exists as an irreducible object. What is an impression? When I observe an apple, for instance, I have an impression of the apple. When I close my eyes and think about the apple, I have an idea of apple. The difference between an impression and an idea is that the impression is more vivid than the idea. An idea is a pale copy of an impression. We believe that an apple exists, even if we are not observing it, because the idea of the apple is derived from the impression of the apple that I acquired when I saw it. We believe, however, that a unicorn does not exist, although we have an idea of unicorn, because we do not have an impression of unicorn from which the idea of unicorn is derived. In simple terms, we have not observed a unicorn, so we cannot say that unicorn exists. So if we do not have an impression of something, we cannot say that that thing exists. Hume contends that we do not have an impression of the mind:

> For from what impression cou'd this idea be deriv'd? This question 'tis impossible to answer without a manifest contradiction and absurdity; and yet 'tis a question, which must necessarily be answer'd, if we wou'd have the idea of self pass for clear and intelligible. (Hume, 1888/1978: 251)

What Hume means by 'self' is the mind. So his point is that since we do not have an impression of the mind, we have no reason for thinking that it exists as an irreducible object.

It might be objected, however, that we have an impression of the mind when we introspect our mind, i.e., when our mind observes itself. Hume replies that introspection reveals only this or that idea, but not the mind:

For my part, when I enter most intimately into what I call myself I always stumble on some particular perception or other, of heat or cold, light or shade, love or hatred, pain or pleasure. I never can catch myself at any time without a perception, and never can observe anything but the perception. (Hume, 1888/1978: 251)

We do not encounter the mind. So what we think of the mind is nothing but a bundle of ideas and impressions. There is no mind over and above the bundle of ideas.

To refute Hume's argument, we need only ask, "What am I that enter most intimately into what I call myself?" Is it my mind as something over and above a collection of ideas? Or is it my mind as merely a collection of ideas? If the former is the case, then Hume's argument is self-defeating. The premise of the argument states that the mind exists as something over and above a collection of ideas, while the conclusion of the argument states that the mind as something over and above a collection of ideas does not exist. If the latter is the case, then it is not clear whether it makes sense to say that a collection of ideas stumble upon ideas. How can a set of ideas observe ideas?

9. The Identity Theory

The identity theory was propounded by J. J. C. Smart (1959). It holds that a mental state is identical with a brain state. Put rigorously, a mental state is reducible to a brain state. For example, pain is reducible to C-fiber stimulation. C-fiber stimulation is a brain event, being a physical event occurring in a brain. Neuroscientists discovered that whenever we feel pain, C-fiber stimulates in our brain. The identity theory maintains that pain just is C-fiber stimulation. That is, pain, on close examination, turns out to be C-fiber stimulation just as water turned out to be H_2O. Pain and C-fiber stimulation are not separate events. They are one and the same event, just as superman and Clark Kent are. To say that pain is reducible to C-fiber firing does not mean that pain is eliminated from people's minds. Pain still exists even if it is reducible to C-fiberfiring, just as water still exists even if it is reducible to H_2O.

Some scientists and philosophers are attracted to the identity theory.

Francis Crick (1916-2004), a Nobel laureate, claims that our mental states "are in fact no more than the behavior of a vast assembly of nerve cells and their associated molecules" (1994: 3). Patricia Churchland, a philosopher, argues that "explanatory power, coherence and economy will favor the hypothesis that awareness just is some pattern of activity in neurons" (1997: 133).

Is the mind extended? Identity theorists' answer is yes because for them, what we call the mind is the brain, and the brain is extended. Therefore, the mind is extended. What should psychologists do to know the mind? Identity theorists say that psychologists only need to study the brain because what we call the mind is nothing but the brain. By studying the brain, we can understand the mind. A perfect neuroscience will give us the complete understanding of the mind in the future.

Why should we accept the identity theory? The following four arguments can be presented for it. First, Ockham's razor favors it over dualism. The identity theory is a form of materialism. Materialism is the view that all that exists is physical. Dualism, in contrast, claims that there are two kinds of things: the mind and the body. So the ontology of the identity theory is simpler than that of dualism.

Second, there is growing success in neuroscience at unraveling the neural correlates of mental states.

One-to-One Correlations

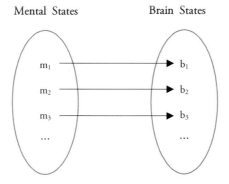

Scientists discovered, for instance, that a material called beta amyloid in our brain is responsible for Alzheimer's disease. If we get rid of the material, we will not contract the disease. Researchers also discovered that serial killers' brain waves are different from those of people who are not serial killers. If neuroscience is completed, we will discover all the one-to-one correlations between mental states and brain states, and neuroscientists will know what people think just by observing their brain states. So it is tempting to identify a mental state with a brain state.

Third, the identity theory has its own response to the mind-body problem: how the mind and the body can causally affect each other. Suppose that the mind is not extended, as dualism claims. Then, it is not clear how the mind can causally affect the body. To say that the mind causally affects the body violates the principle of conservation of mass-energy. The identity theory's solution to the mind-body problem is that the mind can causally affect the body because the mind is reducible to the brain, and the brain can causally affect the body. It is not mysterious how the brain causally affects the body. There can be a physical explanation of how the brain moves our muscles.

Fourth, the identity theory is better than dualism vis-à-vis the problem of other minds. What is the problem of other minds? Dualism proclaims that the mind and the body are distinct entities. We, however, cannot know that other people have minds because we cannot observe their minds. We can only observe their brains and behaviors. So we cannot be certain that others have minds:

> ..you can't directly experience anybody else's mind. You can't have other people's thoughts, feelings, or desires. So, to arrive at the conclusion that other people have minds, you must appeal to certain physical facts. But it seems that those facts can't establish the existence of immaterial minds beyond a reasonable doubt. (Schick and Vaughn, 2010: 96-97).

An MRI only reveals the properties of other people's brains. It does not exhibit their minds. Therefore, we cannot know that they have minds.

Dualists might argue that all brains are similar. In other words, my brain gives rise to a mind, so your brain must give rise to a mind too. Therefore, I am justified in believing that you have a mind.

Skeptics would reply, however, that even if my brain is similar to your brain, and even if I have a mind, there is still a possibility that you do not have a mind. So I cannot know that you have a mind. For all I know, you might be a sophisticated robot. I should be skeptical whether you have a mind or not until I feel what you feel. But I cannot have your feeling. I can only guess about what you feel and only believe that your feeling is similar to mine. But I can never be sure that what I feel coincides with what you feel. So I can never know that you have a mind.

The identity theory's solution to the problem of other minds is that we can observe other people's minds because we can observe their brains. If we observe their brains, we observe their minds, just as if we observe superman, we thereby observe Clark Kent. Thus, we can avoid skepticism about other minds, once we embrace the identity theory.

Let me turn to some objections to the identity theory. First, we conceptualize the mind and the brain differently, i.e., our beliefs about the mind are different from our beliefs about the brain. For example, I believe that my brain has a certain shape and size. But I do not believe that my mind has a certain shape and size. So the mind is not identical with the brain, and they are not one and the same thing. To take another example, people believe that pain is to be avoided. But they do not believe that C-fiber activation is to be avoided. So pain is not identical with C-fiber firing.

Identity theorists could reply that our beliefs about Clark Kent might be different from our beliefs about superman. We might believe that Clark Kent, but not superman, is a newspaper reporter. Yet, Clark Kent is the same person as superman. Similarly, our beliefs about a mental state are different from our beliefs about a brain state. Even so, the mental state might be one and the same as the brain state. Thus, the identity theory stands.

Second, if X and Y are one and the same thing, it is possible to know everything about X by knowing everything about Y, and vice versa. For example, since Clark Kent and superman are one and the same person, we can know everything about Clark Kent by knowing everything about superman, and vice versa. In consequence, if the mind is reducible to the brain as the identity theory asserts, we should be able to know everything about the mind by knowing everything about the brain.

Thomas Nagel (1974) offers an example to argue that complete knowledge about the brain does not guarantee complete knowledge about the mind:

> I want to know what it is like to for a *bat* to be a bat. Yet if I try to imagine this, I am restricted to the resources of my own mind, and those resources are inadequate to the task. (Nagel, 1974: 439)

A bat sends supersonic sonar from its mouth to an object, and can sense the shape of the object by receiving the sonar bounced off from the object. Suppose that we have the perfect neuroscience such that we know all that there is to know about the neurophysiological states of the bat's brain. So we have the complete knowledge about the bat's brain. Even so, we can never know what it is like to be a bat, i.e., we can never have the sensation the bat has when it senses the shape of the object by receiving the sonar from the object. Hence, the mind is distinct from the brain.

Identity theorists could retort that we can know what it is like to be a bat if we have the perfect science and technology in the future. We might be able to devise a machine that could produce in our brain the kind of sensation that the bat has. Nagel would reply that we can never know what it is like to be a bat, even if the bat's sensation is artificially induced in our brain, because we can never be certain that the artificially induced sensation is indeed the sensation that the bat has. We will be able to observe similar chemicals being released in the bat's brain and our brain. But that does not entitle us to say that we *know* what it is like to be a bat. In response, identity theorists could point out that Nagel previously claimed that we can know everything that there is to know about the bat's brain, so he would admit that certainty is not required for a belief to pass for knowledge. Then, identity theorists can say that we can have knowledge about a bat's mind although we may not be certain about it. Thus, we can know what it is like to be a bat. Also, if we can know about other human being's mental state, we can also know about a bat's mental state because they are on the same boat. The best evidence that I have for my belief that my mental state is similar to that of others is that my brain state is similar to their brain state. So if my brain state is similar to a bat's brain state, I am entitled to say that I know what it is like to be a bat.

Third, recall that the identity theory claims that a mental state is reducible to a brain state, just as water is reducible to H_2O. For example, pain is reducible to C-fiber stimulation. The theory implies that where there is pain, there is C-fiber stimulation, just as where there is water, there is H_2O. If C-fiber stimulation does not obtain when pain does, we would not say that pain is reducible to C-fiber stimulation, just as if H_2O does not obtain when water does, we would not say that water is reducible to H_2O.

Hilary Putnam (1975) argues that a mental state is not reducible to a brain state because "from what we already know about computers, etc., that whatever the program of the brain may be, it must be physically possible, though not necessarily feasible, to produce something with that same program but quite a different physical and chemical constitution" (Putnam, 1975: 293). Imagine that we have a sophisticated computer. It looks, talks, and behaves exactly like a human being. Its brain, however, is made out of not carbon but silicon. So it does not have C-fiber stimulation. Can it feel pain when it is damaged, as we feel pain when our body is damaged? Our intuitive answer is that it can. But the identity theory says that it cannot on the grounds that it does not have C-fiber stimulation. The conceivability of such a computer shows that pain is not reducible to C-fiber stimulation. Hence, the identity theory is false.

Similarly, David Lewis (1980) imagines a situation in which pain obtains but C-fiber stimulation does not. Suppose that our brains are made out of carbon and that there are Martians whose brains are made out of silicon. Would Martians feel pain as we do when their tissue is damaged? Our intuitive answer is that they would. If the identity theory were true, however, they would not. After all, their brain states are by hypothesis different from our brain states, so there is no such thing as C-fiber stimulation in their brain. If C-fiber stimulation does not occur in their brain, they do not feel pain. The conceivability of such Martians shows that pain is not reducible to C-fiber stimulation. Hence, the identity theory is false.

Putnam and Lewis use different examples to make the same point. That point is that the same kind of mental state is realizable in different kinds of physical states, just as the same software is realizable in different kinds of hardware.

Multiple Realizability Argument

The same kind of mental state can be realized in different kinds of physical states.

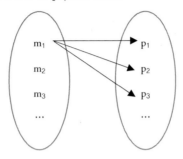

Pain can be realized not only in C-fiber stimulation but also in S-fiber stimulations and in D-fiber stimulations. So pain cannot be identified exclusively with C-fiber stimulation. This argument is called the multiple realizability argument.

How can identity theorists cope with the multiple realizability argument? They can reject Lewis's intuition that Martians can feel pain as earthlings do. After all, we do not have any empirical evidence justifying such a speculative assumption. They dismiss Lewis's argument not simply on the grounds that Martians are imaginary beings but on the grounds that the brain like ours is necessary for there to be the mind like ours. It is not clear how Lewis could prove that Martians would feel pain in the same way we do. If Nagel is right, earthlings can never know what it is like to be a Martian.

Fourth, materialism claims that all that exists is physical. The basis for this claim is that a mental event is reducible to a physical event.

This argument, however, is incorrect. From the fact that a mental event is reducible to a physical event, it does not follow that all that exists is physical. It might be that all that exists is mental because a metal event and a physical event are one and the same event, i.e., a mental event. The reduction might lead to idealism, not to materialism.

Fifth, suppose that X is reducible to Y. The spatiotemporal identity of a reducing item and a reduced item is a requirement for a successful reduction. If X is in some place, so should Y. If X is at a certain point in time, so should Y. Unless this requirement is met, X cannot be reducible to Y. But a brain event is temporally prior to the corresponding mental event (Libet, 1985). The requirement is not met in this case. So a mental state and a brain state cannot be one and the same. This criticism against the identity theory also applies to functionalism.

10. Functionalism

We sometimes define an object not in terms of what it is made out of but in terms of what it does. Think of a digital clock, a water clock, and a sundial (Schick and Vaughn, 2010: 125). They are physically dissimilar but they are all classified as timepieces. Why? What do they have in common? They all tell time. So what makes a clock a clock is not what it is made of, but what it does. In a similar vein, functionalists define a mental state in term of what it does.

Functionalism, developed by Putnam (1967/1975), holds that a mental state is reducible to a functional state. Suppose, for instance, that my finger is cut (stimulus). I feel pain (a mental state), groan (behavioral response), and worry (another mental state) about my finger. A causal relation holds among the stimulus, the response, the pain (one mental state), and the worry (another mental state).

Abnormal Person

Look at what it does!

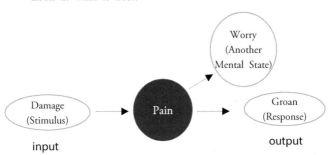

The stimulus causes the pain. The pain causes the groaning and goes into worry. Functionalism defines the pain as that which is caused by the physical damage, and causes the groaning, and goes into the worry. It does not matter whether it is C-fiber stimulation or D-fiber stimulation that performs the causal role. As long as the causal role exists, so does the pain. In other words, the pain exists as long as something physical takes the tissue damage as an input, gives out the groaning behavior as an output, and goes into the worry. So functionalism defines a mental state in terms of the causal relation among a stimulus, a response, and another mental state, not in terms of the material it is made out of. It views the mind as an information processor that accepts information as input, works on it, and produces an output.

What is the difference between functionalism and the identity theory? The identity theory claims a strict one-to-one correspondence between a kind of mental state and a kind of physical state. Suppose that m_1, m_2 and m_3 refer to pain, hunger, and thirst, respectively. They are different kinds of mental states. Suppose also that p_1, p_2 and p_3 refer to carbon, silicon, and iron, respectively. They are different kinds of physical states.

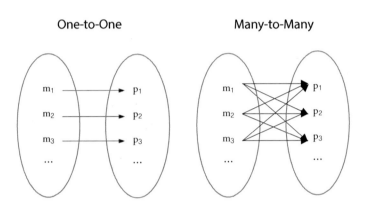

On the one hand, the identity theory holds that m_1 can be realized only in p_1. P_1 can realize only m_1. In other words, m_1 cannot be realized in p_2. P_1 cannot realize m_2. The same is true of m_2, m_3, p_2, and p_3. Functionalism, on the other hand, claims that there is a many-to-many correspondence between mental states and physical states. M_1 can be realized in p_1, p_2, or p_3. P_1 can realize m_1, m_2, or m_3. The same is true of m_2, m_3, m_2, and p_3. Note that the same mental state can be realized in different kinds of physical states, and that the same kind of physical state can realize different kinds of mental states. Recall that according to functionalism, what makes a mental state what it is is not what it is made out of but what it does. As long as p_1, p_2, and p_3 perform the same function, they are the same mental state.

Under the functionalist framework, it is possible for a Martian to feel pain like an earthling, although its brain is silicon-based, and an earthling's brain is carbon-based. Suppose that S-fiber stimulation in a Martian's brain plays the same causal role as C-fiber stimulation does in an earthling's brain. That is, like C-fiber stimulation, S-fiber stimulation takes tissue damage as an input, gives out groaning behavior as an output, and goes into the worry. Then, the Martian feels pain, as the earthling does. After all, what makes a mental state what it is is not what it is made out of but what it does. As long as S-fiber stimulation and C-fiber stimulation do the same thing, they are the same kind of mental states (pains), just as as long as a digital clock and a water clock do the same thing, they are both clocks. Thus, the possibility of Martian pain does not spell trouble to functionalism, although it does to the identity theory. In that sense, functionalism is an improvement upon identity theory.

An implication of functionalism is that the mind can be viewed as a program running on the brain. The mind is to the brain what the software is to the hardware. A mental state can be realized in different physical states, just as the same software can be realized in different kinds of hardware. If the analogy is correct, it should be possible to transfer the mind to a computer. The mind could survive the death of a body, although it always needs another body to be realized in.

Putnam (1981: 80) raises a famous objection to functionalism: the argument from inverted spectrum. Recall that functionalism claims that a mental state is reducible to a functional state. Functional equivalence necessitates mental equivalence. To put it another way, if two people are in the same functional state, they are in the same mental state. Functionalism collapses if it is possible for two people to be in different mental states but the same functional state. Putnam argues that such a possibility obtains. Suppose that Tom looks at the blue sky, has the sensation of blue, says, "The sky is blue" and feels good. Looking at the blue sky is to take information from the world. Saying, "The sky is blue," is to issue a behavioral output. Feeling good is to go into another mental state. The sensation of blue is whatever is caused by looking at the blue sky, causes the verbal utterance, and going into the mental state of feeling good.

Normal Person

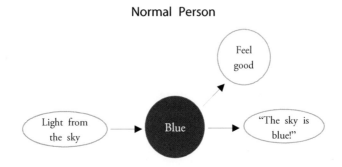

It is possible, so the objection goes, that John has a visual sensation of red instead of blue. His sensation of red is caused by looking at the blue sky, and causes the verbal utterance "The sky is blue." It goes into another mental state of feeling good.

Abnormal Person

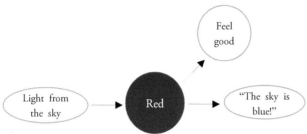

John and Tom are in the same functional state, but in different mental states. This should be impossible, if functionalism is true. But it is possible, so functionalism is false. The upshot of this objection is that functional equivalence does not entail mental equivalence. That is, even if two physical states are functionally identical, it does not necessarily follow that they are the same kind of mental states. So a mental state is not reducible to a functional state.

Study Questions

1. Why is it that I can doubt that a book in on the table, but I cannot doubt that I have a mind?

2. State and criticize Descartes's three distinctions between the mind and the matter.

3. On the one hand, Descartes claims that the mind does not take up space. On the other hand, he asserts that the mind and the body causally interact with each other. Are these two claims compatible or incompatible? What is your position?

4. What is substance dualism? What is Descartes's argument for it? Is there any problem with the argument?

5. What does epiphenomenalism claim? Why would one endorse it? Do you accept or reject it? Justify your answer.

6. What does it mean to say that X is reducible to Y?

7. State idealism and give an argument for it.

8. State Hume's bundle theory of mind, an argument to support it,

and a criticism against it.

9. State the identity theory, using the concept of reduction and an example. State an argument for it and then an argument against it. Do you accept or reject the identity theory? If you accept it, try to come up with an additional argument to support it, and try to refute the objections leveled against it. If you reject it, criticize the arguments for it, and try to come up with an additional objection. Be sure to provide an example to demonstrate an abstract idea.

10. Repeat Question 10, using functionalism instead of identity theory.

CHAPTER

05

Epistemology

Knowledge is power. Scientists pursue knowledge. Physicists seek physical knowledge, biologists biological knowledge, and psychologists psychological knowledge. But scientists do not ask what knowledge is, although they seek it. It is the realm of philosophy to raise and answer questions about knowledge. The field of philosophy devoted to the study of knowledge is called epistemology.

Consider the following statements. Some of them are knowable; others are unknowable or controversial.

(1) Snow is white.
(2) Dinosaurs existed.
(3) A unicorn exists.
(4) 1+1=2.

We can say that we *know* that snow is white as long as we can observe it. It follows that as long as we can see something, we *know* that it exists. But what about (2)? We cannot observe dinosaurs. But we know that they existed because we can observe their fossils. It follows that we can know that something exists even if we cannot observe it. What about (3)? Why is it that we cannot say that we know that a unicorn exists? What about (4)? We cannot observe 1 or 2, although we can count on our fingers. This chapter answers these questions.

1. Plato's Analysis of Knowledge

What is knowledge? Under what conditions can we say that we know that p? (P is a proposition or a claim.) Consider the following sentence:

(A) I know that the Earth is flat.

A contradiction is involved in asserting (A). We cannot know that the Earth is flat because it is false that the Earth is flat. So when I know that p, p must be true. In other words, I cannot know that p unless it is true. It follows that truth is an ingredient of knowledge. There are other ingredients of knowledge. Consider the following sentence:

(B) I know that the Earth is round, but I do not believe that the Earth is round.

There is a contradiction is in asserting (B). The oddity of asserting (B) shows that a belief is another essential condition of knowledge.

When you know that p, you believe that p. You cannot know that p unless we believe it. Now, consider the following sentence:

> (C) I know that the Earth is round, but I do not have evidence to believe that the earth is round.

(C) is tricky. Some say that it is not a contradiction, while Plato says that it is. According to Plato, sufficient evidence is another essential condition of knowledge, i.e., in order for us to know that p, we must possess good evidence for it. Thus, according to Plato, knowledge is a justified true belief.

We have many beliefs. They can be divided into true beliefs and false beliefs. True beliefs correspond to states of affairs. False beliefs do not.

Justified true beliefs (knowledge)	Justified false beliefs
Unjustified true beliefs	Unjustified false beliefs

True beliefs can in turn be divided into justified true beliefs and unjustified true beliefs. False beliefs can in turn be divided into justified false beliefs and unjustified false beliefs.

Here are some examples. Suppose that I believe that snow is white. It is true that snow is white. I have perceptual evidence that snow is white. Then, I have a justified true belief that snow is white, i.e., I know that snow is white.

Suppose that I make a guess as to whether there is life outside of the Earth. That is, I do not have any evidence, but I believe that there is life outside of the Earth. Suppose also that it is true that there is life outside of the Earth. In that case, what I have is an unjustified true belief. In plain language, an unjustified true belief is a lucky guess.

Can there be a justified false belief? The answer is yes. We might believe that p, and we have good evidence for p. Still, it is false. For example, our ancestors believed that the Earth is at rest and that the heavens are in motion. They had good evidence for the belief. Look at the night sky. It appears that the heavens are in motion and that the Earth is at rest. A stone thrown upwards lands in its original place. So our ancestors were justified in believing that the Earth is at rest and that the heavens are in motion. But this justified belief was false. So we can say at best that a justified belief is *likely* to be true. Justification does not guarantee truth, so a justified belief might be false.

Suppose that I believe that a unicorn exists, even though I do not have evidence that they exist, and that it is false that a unicorn exists. My belief in unicorns is an unjustified false belief.

There is a significant difference between knowledge and belief. Suppose that your opponents in an intellectual discussion express their belief, but do not present any evidence for it. You are entitled to reject it. Suppose, however, that they justify their belief with evidence and that it is true. Then, what they have is knowledge, and you have no choice but to accept it.

2. Analytic vs. Synthetic

How does mathematics differ from physics and biology? How does knowledge of mathematics differ from knowledge of physics or biology? Answers to these questions can be found in the distinction between analytic and synthetic statements:

Analytic Statements
- A bachelor is unmarried.
- If John is a physicist, he is a scientist.

Synthetic Statements
- An apple is red.
- The Earth is round.

Consider the statement: A bachelor is unmarried. It is true. But it would be false, if 'bachelor' means a married adult male. So the meanings of the words in the statement are what makes the statement true. In this sense, an analytic statement is true or false in virtue of the way a language is used. In other words, it is true or false by what the words in it mean.

A true analytic statement is true no matter what happens in the world. Suppose that all bachelors died, so there are no bachelors in the world. Even so, it is true that a bachelor is unmarried. It is not the case that a true analytic statement becomes false as the world changes. In this sense, an analytic statement is true or false independently of the way the world is. So a linguistic meaning is the sole determiner of whether an analytic statement is true or false. Put differently, a linguistic meaning is the sole truth-maker for an analytic statement.

But how about the statement 'An apple is red'? The statement is true. But it would be false, if 'apple' means snow, the white cold stuff on the ground. After all, snow is white. What is true would be the statement that an apple is white. So the meanings of words in the statement make the statement true. In this sense, a synthetic statement is true or false partly by virtue of the way a language is used. To put it another way, it is true or false partly by what words mean.

There is another way for the synthetic statement to be false. It would be false, even if 'apple' means apple, if a genetic mutation occurs and all apples become white. Then, what is true would be the statement that an apple is white. So the world is partly what makes the synthetic statement true or false. A true synthetic statement might become false as the world changes. In this sense, a synthetic statement is true or false partly in virtue of the way the world is. So both a linguistic meaning and the world jointly determine whether a synthetic statement is true or false. To put it differently, a linguistic meaning and the world are the truth-makers for a synthetic statement.

A quick way to distinguish analytic from synthetic statements is to ask: Does the world make a statement true or false? Or does the truth-value of a statement change as the world changes? If the answers are yes, the statement is synthetic. If the answers are no, the statement is synthetic.

An analytic statement does not contain information about the world but a synthetic statement does. An analytic statement does not tell us anything about the world. It is empty of factual content. It is not a description of the way the world is. It is not true of the world even if it is true. It is trivially true, if true. A synthetic statement, in contrast, does tell us something about the world. It is a description of the way the world is. A true synthetic statement is true of the world.

This fundamental difference between analytic and synthetic statements yields the following derivative difference. We do not have to observe the world to know whether an analytic statement is true or false. We can see the truth or the falsity of an analytic statement, only if we know what the statement means. For instance, if we know what 'bachelor' and 'unmarried' mean as a competent English speaker, then we can just see that it is true that a bachelor is unmarried. By contrast, we have to observe the world to know whether a synthetic statement is true or false. For example, we cannot know that an apple is red just by grasping the meanings of the words 'apple' and 'red.'

An analytic statement is not subject to empirical refutation, whereas a synthetic statement is. It is of no use to try to refute an analytic statement with observational evidence. For example, you cannot refute the statement that a bachelor is unmarried with observational evidence. It would be pointless to search the world for a married bachelor. In contrast, you can refute a synthetic statement with observational evidence. It makes sense to search the world with a view to refuting the statement that an apple is red. If you come across a white apple, the synthetic statement that an apple is red is refuted.

How about a mathematical statement '1+1=2'? Is it analytic or synthetic? According to the empiricist view in philosophy of mathematics, a mathematical statement is analytic. The truth-value of the statement 1+1=2 is not affected by what happens in the world. Suppose that a lion and a rabbit are put in the same cage and that the lion eats the rabbit. Even so, it is true that 1+1=2. It is not the case that the mathematical statement becomes false as the lion eats the rabbit. So it is of no use to try to refute it with empirical evidence. A mathematical statement is not subject to refutation by empirical evidence. It is not surprising that there is no laboratory in departments of mathematics, but there are laboratories in departments of physics or in departments of biology. The empiricist view, however, has a problem. If a mathematical statement is empty of factual content, it is not clear why mathematics is useful in physics.

There is a problem with the analytic-synthetic distinction. There are cases in which it is hard to determine whether a statement is analytic or synthetic. Consider the statement 'Everything green is extended.' It is not clear whether it is analytic or synthetic (Quine, 1994: 32). Consider also the statement 'A female is a creature that gives birth.' We might take this statement to be analytic. It is, however, a false synthetic statement, given that zoology tells us that male seahorses give birth. Consider also the following tricky statements:

(a) F=ma.

(b) If you study hard, you will pass the exam.

(a) is Newton's second law of motion. Is it a definition of 'force'? Or it is a description of the way the world is? If it is the definition, it is an analytic statement containing no information about the world. If it is the description, it is a synthetic statement subject to empirical refutation. How about (b)? Can we think of a state of affairs which would refute it? If not, it is an analytic statement.

3. A Priori vs. A Posteriori

Recall that according to Plato, knowledge is a justified true belief. As we have seen in Chapter 1, a belief is a mental state that can be true or false, a belief is true when it corresponds to the world, and it is false when it does not correspond to the world. It is now time to talk about justification. What is a source of justification? Where does it come from? Consider the following statements:

(1) An apple is red.

The Earth is round.

(2) A bachelor is unmarried.

If John is a physicist, he is a scientist.

I am justified in believing that an apple is red. 'Being justified' simply means possessing good evidence. A justified belief is likely to be true. Then, what is the source of justification for the belief that an apple is red? It is experience. I am observing the apple, or I have observed the apple. My perceptual evidence supports the belief that an apple is red. I would not be justified in believing so, if I have not observed an apple in my life. In this sense, (1) is a posteriori. A statement is a posteriori when the justification for it comes from experience.

I am also justified in believing that a bachelor is unmarried. But the justification for it does not come from experience. After all, I am justified in believing that a bachelor is unmarried even before I observe any bachelor. Then, what is the source of justification in this case? It is reason, which is also called rationality, mind, intellect, understanding, cognition, and intuition in philosophy.

What is reason? So far as I know, there is no precise definition in the philosophy literature. I would say that reason is a cognitive faculty, the power of mind, which makes analytic, mathematical, and synthetic a priori judgments possible. In plain English, reason enables us to think. Reason is in contrast with sense. We can perceive an object because we have the cognitive faculty, perception.

All synthetic truths, it seems, are knowable a posteriori. A synthetic statement needs to be justified with observations in order to be transformed into knowledge. This claim is controversial, though. Empiricists affirm it, while rationalists deny it.

The distinction between a priori and a posteriori statements is different from the distinction between analytic and synthetic statements.

The distinction between analytic and synthetic statements is an answer to the question: What makes a statement true or false? If a statement is rendered true or false solely by the way a language is used, it is analytic. If it is rendered true or false by the way a language is used and by the way the world is, it is synthetic. In contrast, the distinction between a priori and a posteriori statements is an answer to the question: What is the source of justification for a statement? If the source is reason, the statement is a priori. If the source is experience, the statement is a posteriori.

4. Empiricism vs. Rationalism

Empiricism holds that all knowledge about the world comes from experience. We cannot know about the world unless we observe it, i.e., thinking alone cannot reveal anything about the world. If we know something without observing the world, that thing has nothing to do with the world, i.e., it does not contain information about the world. In short, all a priori knowledge is analytic.

In contrast, rationalism claims that some knowledge about the world comes from reason. Thus, we can know something about the world even before we observe it, i.e., thinking alone can tell us something about the world. In short, some a priori knowledge is synthetic. Rationalists provide the following examples as synthetic a priori knowledge:

<u>Putative Synthetic A Priori Knowledge</u>
- Every event has a cause.

- Every physical object is in space and time.

- Everything that has shape has color.

- Two objects cannot be in the same place at the same time.

- 1+1=2.

These statements, rationalists claim, are true of the world. Yet, justifications for them come not from experience but from reason. In other words, we know that they are true even before we perceive the world.

Let's discuss Kant's case for rationalism. Suppose that we wear red sunglasses and that we somehow know that we wear them. Then, we can be certain, even before we observe the world, that objects will appear to be red. Kant claims that we are born with assumptions like "Every event has a cause" and "Every physical object exists in space and time." They are genetically hardwired into our mind. We look at the world through these assumptions. So we inevitably interpret an event as having a cause, and a physical object as existing in space and time. As a result, an event inescapably appears to be caused by another, and a physical object inevitably appears to exist in space and time. Therefore, the justification for the aforementioned assumptions comes from reason.

Empiricists could reply, however, that these assumptions are nothing but empirical generalizations. We observe some instances in which an event has a cause, and some instances in which a physical object exists in space and time. We generalize that every event has a cause and that every physical object exists in space and time. Hence, justifications for the general assumptions come from experience, and they are synthetic a posteriori knowledge.

Kant would retort that there is a significant difference between the following two inferences:

(a) Some crows are black. Therefore, all crows are black.
(b) Some events have causes. Therefore, every event has a cause.

We are not certain that (a) is correct, but we are certain that (b) is correct. Why are we sure of (b), but not of (a)? Kant would say that the assumption that every event has a cause is genetically hardwired in our mind, but the assumption that all crows are black is not.

Suppose that your car is broken and that you take it to a mechanic. After inspecting it, the mechanic says that there is not a cause of the mechanical failure. The car just does not run. Since there is not a cause of the failure, there is no way to fix the car. How would we respond to the mechanic? We would say to him that there is a cause; he has not yet found it. What are the grounds for this conviction? Kant's answer is that we are looking at the world through the assumption that every event has a cause.

Let's go over Descartes's case for rationalism. He claims that we possess some innate concepts. We acquire innate concepts independently of experience, and yet they have corresponding objects and properties in the world. We have, for instance, an idea of chiliagon, a thousand-sided figure (Moser, Mulder, and Trout, 1998: 104). That idea is not empirically acquired because we cannot visualize that figure. Furthermore, we can make inferences, using the concept of chiliagon. For example, we can infer that a chiliagon has more sides than a square. The claim is not based on sensory experience, for we cannot even visualize a chiliagon. We use reason, not the senses, when we make such inferences. It follows that we can know about the world without having observational evidence, i.e., synthetic a priori knowledge is possible.

Two replies are possible from the perspective of empiricism. First, it is false that the concept of chiliagon is innate. It is derived from such simple concepts as the concept of triangle and the concept of square. Descartes might object that the concept of chiliagon is still innate because we cannot visualize the figure. I reply that the inability to visualize something does not mean that the concept of that thing is innate. We cannot visualize, for example, all swans in the universe. Even so, the concept of all swans is not innate but empirical. Thus, not being visualizable does not entail being innate.

Second, it is one thing for a concept to be innate; it is another for it to correspond to an object in the world. Empiricists would say that the mathematical statement that a chiliagon has more sides than a square is not synthetic but analytic. It is not true of the world. So the alleged synthetic a priori knowledge is analytic a priori knowledge. Descartes's case for rationalism fails.

5. Plato's Theory of Forms

Suppose that we draw a triangle on the board and get rid of the ink mark with an eraser. Although you have erased the ink mark, you have not erased the triangle; the triangle still exists. Where does it exist? According to Plato (Jones, 1970: 124-146), it exists in the world of being. He distinguishes the world of being (or the world of reality) from the world of becoming (the world of appearance).

The world of becoming is inhabited by physical objects. Consider a physical object, say, an apple. It is mutable, i.e., it is subject to change. It is temporal and spatial, i.e., it exists in time and space. So it makes sense to say that it exists now and here. It is ephemeral, i.e., it exists only for a certain period of time. It is destructible, i.e., it can be cut into pieces. It is sensible, i.e., we can identify it with five senses.

In contrast, the world of being is inhabited by Forms. What are Forms? Consider, for example, that there are many beautiful objects: a flower, a landscape, and a girl. Why are they beautiful? According to Plato, they are beautiful because they resemble and participate in the Form of Beauty. A stone is not beautiful because it does not resemble the Form of Beauty. There is a fundamental difference between the beautiful things in the world of becoming and the Form of Beauty in the world of being. Beautiful things are mutable, but the Form of Beauty is immutable. Since beautiful things change, they are less real. Since the Form of Beauty does not change, it is real. Consider apple and a grape. Why is an apple a fruit? Why is a grape a fruit? According to Plato, an apple is a fruit because it participates in the Form of Fruit. A grape is a fruit because it also participates in the Form of Fruit. An apple and a grape are mutable and hence less real, whereas the Form of Fruit is immutable and hence real. Forms have other properties that physical objects do not have. Forms are non-temporal and non-spatial, i.e., they exist outside of time and space. They are indestructible. They are intelligible, i.e., we can understand them with the use of reason. They cannot be perceived with the senses.

Plato claims that a mathematical object is a Form. So a mathematical object has all the properties of a Form. A mathematical object is immutable. It is not the case, for example, that a triangle will become a square. Nor is it the case that 1+2 will become 4. A mathematical object is non-temporal and non-spatial. So it is wrong to say that 1+2 *was* 3 and that 1+2=3 *here*. A mathematical object is indestructible and intelligible. We cannot observe it with five senses.

Plato's Theory of Forms is useful for distinguishing a sentence from a proposition. A proposition is an abstract entity that is either true or false. It is expressed by a declarative sentence. Consider the following two sentences:

'The Earth is round.'
'지구는 둥글다.'

One is English; the other is Korean. So they are different sentences, but they express the same proposition. A proposition exists in the world of being, whereas a sentence exists in the world of becoming. The sentence can be perceived by a sense organ. You can hear the sentence uttered by your friend, and you can see the sentence written on a board. But the proposition cannot be perceived by sense. It can only be grasped by reason.

Why should we believe that Forms exist in the world of being? Let's discuss Plato's two arguments for the existence of Forms. According to the first argument:

A mathematical object exists independently of human conception.
It does not exist in the world of becoming.
∴ It exists in the world of being.

For example, a triangle has many properties. One of them is that the sum of the three angles is 180 degrees. Do we invent this property or discover it? In other words, does the property come into existence because we thought of it? Or did it exist prior to that? We believe that we discovered the property. Therefore, it exists in the world of being.

For Plato, a mathematical statement is synthetic. The statement '1+1=2' is true of a mathematical fact in the world of being. It is true because it corresponds to the mathematical fact in the world of being. We identify the mathematical fact not with physical eyes but with mental eyes, viz., reason. In this sense, Plato was a rationalist.

For empiricists, however, what is real is what you can observe. The world of becoming is the real world. There is no such thing as the world of being. Then, why is it true that 1+1=2? For empiricists, a mathematical statement is analytic, meaning that it is true or false by virtue of what it means and independently of the way the world is. It is not the case that a mathematical fact renders it true. Its truth does not consist in the correspondence with a fact.

Plato's second argument for the existence of Forms can be summarized in the following standard form:

> What we know about exists. (Knowledge entails existence.)
> We know about equality.
> ∴Equality exists.

Let me flesh out the first premise. We know, for example, that the Earth is round. But we cannot know that the Earth is flat. It is a contradiction to say that we know that the Earth is flat. We can know only about what exists. We cannot know about what does not exist. Thus, if we know about something, that thing necessarily exists.

Let me turn to the second premise. Consider two coins. They are unequal, i.e., that are not identical, given that there is a slight difference between them, although the slight difference is not readily perceptible. We know that they are unequal because we know about equality. After all, if we do not know about equality, how can we know that the two coins are unequal? So equality exists.

> Equality does not exist in the world of becoming.
> ∴ Equality exists in the world of being.

The premise of this argument seems to be true. No two things are equal in the physical universe. So equality does not exist in the world of becoming. It must, then, exist in the world of being.

In response to this argument, empiricists would say that equality is fictional. It is merely a mental construct. It is not the case that equality exists in the world of being. The concept of equality is merely a mental instrument for making judgments about physical objects, just as a mathematical object is merely a mental instrument for making a judgment about a physical object.

Let me introduce three classic objections to Plato's theory of Forms. First, there seems to be a wide gulf between the world of being and the world of becoming. How can a human being, a spatial and temporal being, understand something that is non-temporal and non-spatial? Plato claims that we have the cognitive faculty, reason. We can understand Forms through the use of reason. But it is not clear how we existing in the world of becoming can grasp Forms in the world of being. After all, there is no causal relationship between the world of being and us. Plato must have elaborated upon the story of how our mind can comprehend Forms.

Second, Plato claims that a physical object belongs to a certain kind because it participates in the corresponding form. For example, a girl is beautiful because she participates in the Form of Beauty. Why does she participate in the Form of Beauty? Plato has no choice but to say that she participates in the Form of Beauty because she participates in the Form of Participation. This answer, however, amounts to explaining participation in terms of participation, which is circular. An explanation is circular when something is explained in terms of that very thing.

Third, Plato claims that a girl is less beautiful whereas the Form of Beauty is really beautiful. But why is the Form of Beauty really beautiful? He has no choice but to say that it is really beautiful because it participates in the higher Form of Beauty. This answer, however, invites a further question: Why is the higher Form of Beauty is beautiful? Thus, Place faces the task of explaining why a girl is beautiful without running into the problem of infinite regress.

6. Theories of Justification

Under what condition is a belief justified? This question has led epistemologists to three theories of justification: foundationalism, coherentism, and reliabilism. Let me briefly summarize what they assert about the condition under which a belief is justified.

According to foundationalism, there are two sorts of justified beliefs: basic and nonbasic. Basic beliefs are mental beliefs, the ones about our own mental states. For example, the belief that I seem to see a red apple is a mental belief. Nonbasic beliefs are physical beliefs, the ones about physical objects. For example, the belief that an apple is red is a physical belief. The physical belief is justified because it probably, but not necessarily, follows from the mental belief that I seem to see a red apple. In other words, if I seem to see a red apple, it is likely that there is a red apple, hence my belief that an apple is red is justified. The mental belief supports the physical belief not with 100% probability but with less than 100% probability. Foundationalism says that the basic belief is self-justified. That is, it does not owe its justification to other belief. A nonbasic belief is justified if and only if it is well-founded upon basic beliefs, meaning that it probably follows from basic beliefs. The belief, for example, that a unicorn exists is not well-built upon a mental belief, so it is not a justified belief.

Coherentism offers a different story. It holds that a belief is justified if and only if it coheres with other beliefs. Consider the following system of beliefs:

(p) All current organisms have descended from a common ancestor.

(q) All current organisms use the same genetic code.

(r) A human embryo and a pig's embryo are similar initially, but they become dissimilar as they grow.

According to coherentism, (p) is justified because it coheres with (q) and (r). So are (q) and (r). On the coherentist account, there are no such things as self-justified beliefs. A belief, mental or physical, is justified if and only if it coheres with other beliefs, mental or physical. Thus, the fundamental difference between foundationalism and coherentism is that foundationalism distinguishes between basic and nonbasic beliefs, whereas coherentism does not.

Reliabilism (Goldman, 1979) offers yet another story of how a belief is justified. It claims that a belief is justified if and only if it is produced by a reliable cognitive process. A reliable cognitive process is one that produces a high frequency of true beliefs. Suppose that I observe a book on the desk and that my mind is functioning properly. Then, my belief that there is a book on the desk is justified. What would be an example of belief that is produced by an unreliable cognitive process? Our mind consists of a bunch of cognitive systems. One of them is a face recognition system. It is devoted to recognizing faces. If it breaks down, we have a problem recognizing faces. We cannot even recognize our family member's face, although we can recognize parts of the face. A belief formed by such a malfunctioning cognitive system is not justified.

7. Social Epistemology

According to Alvin Goldman (1999: 4-5), traditional epistemology is an attempt to shed light on the relationship between a single cognizer and the world. It focuses on the cognitive operation of a single person in isolation from others. Under this tradition, epistemologists raise and answer questions like "Can we know about the world?," "What is the source of knowledge?," and "Is perception reliable?" The field of epistemology that they established is called individual epistemology. In 1980s, however, some epistemologists became interested in the social interactions between cognitive agents, having realized that the significant portion of our knowledge about the world comes from the interactions with our cognitive colleagues. They are concerned with questions like "How should cognitive agents interact with one another to acquire knowledge?," "What social practice is good at producing knowledge?," and "What modification is required to produce more knowledge?" The field of epistemology that they founded is called social epistemology.

There are diverse social practices in science, law, politics, and education. Goldman's social epistemology evaluates them in terms of their tendencies to produce knowledge. Social practices that promote true beliefs are regarded as good; social practices that promote false beliefs are regarded as bad. Let me summarize how Goldman (Goldman, 1999, Chapter 9) assesses some practices in law. This will give us a glimpse into social epistemology. There are two legal traditions: common law and civil law. Which tradition is better at producing true judgments as to whether a defendant is guilty or not guilty? To answer this question, we first need to go over some key differences between the two legal systems. In the common law system, partisan lawyers gather evidence, are allowed to meet witnesses outside of the court, prepare expert witnesses, and dominate the court with interrogations and argumentations. In addition, a jury decides guilt or innocence. In the civil law system, a neutral judge gathers evidence, prepares expert witnesses, and serves as investigator and decision-maker. Lawyers are allowed neither to meet witnesses outside trial nor to interrogate witnesses at trial. In addition, the judge decides guilt or innocence.

Goldman evaluates these practices in terms of the tendency to produce true beliefs. Let me summarize here what he says about partisan counsels' crucial role in the common law system. The justification for this crucial role is that the best way for the court to discover truths is to have each side of the litigation strive as hard as it can to come up with evidence favorable to that side. As long as the judge is neutral, the goal of arriving at the truth will be served. Goldman (1999: 296) objects that in pretrial phases, partisan lawyers create or change the evidence rather than simply interpret or debate it. A witness who desires to help the lawyer unconsciously molds his story. Lawyers try to hide the defects of their witness. On cross-examination, an experienced lawyer tarnishes the image of the witness who gives testimony disadvantageous to his client, although he knows that the witness is telling the truth. Finally, trial outcomes depend heavily on the skills of the prosecuting and defense lawyers (1999: 298).

Another key difference between the common law system and the civil law system is that the judgment of guilt or innocence is made by a jury in the common law system and by judges in the civil law system. Why is such an important judgment made by people who are not legal experts? The justification for the practice is that jury service is an important facet of self-government, a bulwark against central authority, and a means of educating the citizenry (Goldman, 1999: 311). In some cases, however, judges and juries disagree (Goldman, 1999: 312). So a study needs to be conducted to see how accurate laypeople are in deciding guilt or innocence.

Study Questions

1. For Plato, what is knowledge? Provide examples of an unjustified true belief and a justified false belief.

2. Define analytic and synthetic statements, and provide examples. For empiricists, why is it that 1+1=2 even if a lion eats a rabbit?

3. Define a priori and a posteriori statements, and provide examples.

4. How do empiricism and rationalism differ? Discuss Kant's case for rationalism.

5. For Plato, is a mathematical statement analytic or synthetic? What is a Form? Discuss Plato's argument for the existence of Forms.

6. What are the three theories of justification? Which one is the best? Defend your answer.

7. State the key differences between the common law system and the civil-law system. Which system is better in producing true beliefs as to whether a defendant is guilty or not guilty?

CHAPTER

06

Evolutions

1. Evolutionary Theory

The tree of life and the principle of natural selection are the main frames of evolutionary theory. They jointly constitute its core. The theory of evolution is not refuted as long as they remain unscathed. To use an analogy, a building does not collapse even if a small brick is destroyed. It only collapses when its main frame is destroyed. Likewise, the theory of evolution will fall only when these two main ideas are falsified. Let me explicate them one by one.

The tree of life is a description of genealogical facts. It shows how organisms, past and present, are related to one another. It specifies which species have descended from which others, and which species have gone extinct. Darwin thought that "present and past species form a *single tree*" (Sober, 1993: 8). Thus, the tree of life is like a family tree, but for all living things. What follows from the tree of life is that all current terrestrial organisms share a common ancestor: single-celled organisms. Contemporary biology postulates that different kinds of organisms emerged in the following order: organic compounds, self-replicating molecules, single-celled organisms, algae, marine invertebrates, marine vertebrates, fish, amphibians, reptiles, dinosaurs, mammals, birds, and primates (Kitcher, 1982: 27-28). This shows that organisms have evolved from simple forms to complex forms.

Natural selection, on the other hand, describes the main mechanism by which species have evolved. Let me first use an example to illustrate the principle of natural selection. Mice today can run fast. Why can they run fast? In the past, mice on the average could not run as fast as current mice can. Some mice were born with the ability to run fast. There were predators, there was not enough food in the environment, and the ability to run fast was sexually appealing. Under such circumstances, the fast-running mice had a better chance to survive and reproduce than the slow-running ones. The offspring of the fast-running ones inherited the ability to run fast. Over many generations, all the slow-running mice died out, and only the fast running mice survived. That is why current mice can run fast.

As the above example illustrates, natural selection occurs when three conditions are met. First, a variation must occur within the population. Suppose, for instance, that all mice run at the same speed. Then, natural selection on speed cannot occur. Some members must run faster than others for there to be a change, with respect to speed, in the composition of the population of mice in successive generations. Second, the variation must contribute to fitness. Fitness is the likelihood of survival and reproduction, i.e., a product of viability and fertility. Unless the ability to run fast makes some difference to the survival and reproduction of mice, there would be no change in the composition of the population in successive generations. If the ability to run fast conferred no advantage on survival and reproduction, the fast-running mice and the slow-running ones would have an equal chance of survival and reproduction. Third, the variation must be heritable. Even if fast-running mice are fitter than slow-running ones, there would not be a change in the composition of the population in successive generations, unless the ability to run fast is passed onto the next generation. In short, natural selection occurs when there is heritable variation in fitness (Sober, 1993: 9). Variations occur at random, but natural selection as a whole is not a random process. Only fit organisms *tend to* survive and reproduce.

Biologists use the tree of life and the principle of natural selection to explain biological phenomena: human eyes, giraffes' long necks, and so forth. Why do we have eyes? In the past, organisms did not have eyes. A variation occurred to a group of organisms. Some were born with a primitive organ which was sensitive to light. This organ enabled the organisms to sense whether the environment they were in was dark or bright, and if bright, whether there was an object in front of them or not. There were predators, and there were not enough resources around, so there was a struggle for survival and reproduction. Besides, the organ contributed to the sexual appeal. Because they could sense the presence of predators or food, and because they were more sexually appealing, the organisms with the organ had a better chance to survive and reproduce than the ones without it. As a result, the former defeated the latter in the relentless competition to survive and reproduce. The offspring of the former group also had the organ. After many generations, another variation occurred: the progeny were born with a more sophisticated organ than their parents. With the sophisticated organ, they could see black and white. They were better adapted to the environment than those with the less sophisticated organ, excelling in the relentless battle to eat, to avoid being eaten, and to have offspring. Their offspring also had the same organ. Through a series of such variations, the light-sensitive organ developed into eyes, and organisms without eyes died out. That is why we have eyes now.

2. The Evolutions of Mind and Morality

There is a field of psychology called evolutionary psychology, in which psychologists explain mental phenomena in terms of the theory of evolution. Why, for example, do we feel pain when our body is damaged? Evolutionary psychologists answer that in the past, organisms did not feel pain when their tissues were damaged. A variation occurred, i.e., some of their offspring felt pain when their tissue was damaged. They were more likely to survive and reproduce than those who did not feel pain at all. After a series of variations, the organisms capable of feeling pain survived, while others died out. That is why we feel pain when our tissue is damaged.

To take another example, pregnant women suffer from nausea in their early stage of pregnancy. Initially, this mental phenomenon seems to be a mystery from an evolutionary point of view. After all, pregnant women need more nutrients than non-pregnant women. But they take fewer nutrients due to pregnancy nausea. Pregnancy nausea would thus seem to decrease the chance to have healthy babies. So our ancestors who suffered from pregnancy nausea should have perished, but they did not. As a result, most women today suffer from pregnancy nausea. If evolutionary theory is true, pregnancy nausea should not exist. But it exists. So evolutionary theory is false.

Paul Sherman and Samuel Flaxman (2002) give an evolutionary explanation of pregnancy nausea. They say that the "nausea and vomiting of pregnancy is an intricate mechanism that probably evolved to serve a useful function: protecting the pregnant women and embryo from food-borne infections and toxins" (2002: 190). The idea is that unborn babies might be deformed or die, if they are exposed to harmful materials. The food that mothers eat might contain such materials. Babies are safer if they are supplied with the nutrients that are stored in their mothers' bodies, than if they are supplied with the nutrients from the food that mothers just ate. Moreover, embryos do not need many nutrients, although fetuses do, and embryos are more vulnerable to miscarriage than fetuses. Interestingly, pregnant women experience more intense nausea in the early stages of pregnancy than in the late stages. Thus, there is a correlation between the intensity of nausea and the vulnerability of babies. Also, babies born from mothers who experience intense pregnancy nausea are healthier than those born from mothers who experience moderate pregnancy nausea. Thus, pregnancy nausea increases the chance to have healthy babies, and evolutionary theory explains why pregnant women suffer from nausea.

Evolutionary theory can also explain other mental phenomena: hunger, sexual desire, parental love, etc. Why do we feel hunger when our stomach is empty? Why do we feel the sexual desire when we reach adolescence? Why do parents love their children? All these questions can be answered from an evolutionary point of view. The answers suggest that the mind is an advantageous trait, which makes organisms more likely to enjoy longevity and fecundity. Thus, the mind is a product of evolution, having been shaped and molded by the needs of the body over a long period of time. It is a means for the body to survive and reproduce.

There is a field of ethics called evolutionary ethics. Evolutionary ethicists explain morality in terms of evolutionary theory. Consider that we have moral rules, such as "Don't kill others", "Don't steal from others", "Don't commit adultery", "Keep a promise," and "Help the weak." Why do we have such rules? Where did they come from? Theists might maintain that they came down from God. Evolutionary ethicists, however, suggest that moral rules are with us today because they were advantageous for the survival and reproduction of our ancestors. Imagine that there were two groups of people in the distant past. The first group abided by the moral rules, whereas the second group did not. It is clear that the first group had better chance to perpetuate itself than the second group.

An immoral behavior, such as stealing, might be beneficial to a person who commits it in a particular context, but it harms the group the individual belongs to. Natural selection occurs not only at the level of the individual but also at the level of groups. A group which abides by moral rules is more likely to perpetuate itself than a group which does not.

Group selection explains not only the existence of moral rules but also the existence of altruistic behavior and cooperation between members of a group. For example, if wolves attack a group of buffalos, strong male buffalos will form a circle. Female and young buffalos will retreat to the center of the circle. The male buffalos are strong enough to confront the wolves. Imagine that there were two groups of buffalos in the past. Male buffalos of the first group formed a circle to protect their young and female buffalos, but male buffalos of the second group fled from wolves. It is clear that the first group would have had a better chance to survive and reproduce. Altruistic behavior is disadvantageous for altruistic individuals, but it is advantageous for the group. A group with altruists does better in the struggle for existence than a group with only selfish individuals.

3. The Modularity of Mind

There is a neurological syndrome called prosopagnosia. Patients with this syndrome cannot recognize a face, although they can recognize other objects, such as trees and cups. They can even perfectly describe the parts of a face, but cannot recognize even their family member's face. The syndrome suggests that our mind has a cognitive system devoted to recognizing faces and that it is broken. Cognitive scientists call it the face recognition system.

There is another neurological syndrome called autism that usually presents in childhood. Autistic children treat human beings as mindless objects, such as a stone and a car, believing that there is no difference between human beings and inanimate objects. They are not aware that human beings have minds. So they do not ascribe a mental state to other people, and they cannot read others' minds. This syndrome suggests that our mind has a cognitive system devoted to reading others' minds. Cognitive scientists call it the theory of mind module and hypothesize that autistic children's theory of mind module is broken.

Prosopagnosia and autism motivate the modular theory of mind according to which the mind is made up of many modules. A module is a cognitive system that takes an input, processes it, and generates an output. The face recognition system and the theory of mind module are different modules. When you look at your mother's face, your face recognition system takes the visual information about your mother's face as an input, operates on it, and produces the judgment that it is your mother's face. Suppose that your mother smiles. Your theory of mind module takes the visual information about your mother's face as an input, works on it, and produces the judgment that she is happy.

A module has the following four distinctive properties: First, it is fast in processing information. The process is so fast that it is not available to consciousness, i.e., we are not aware of the process of taking the input, working on the input, and giving out the output. When we look at a face, the face recognition system kicks in and processes the information about the face almost instantaneously. It is for this reason that upon seeing a face, we know whose face it is.

Second, the operation of a module is not optional but mandatory. You cannot stop the process of taking an input and giving out an output at will. When you look at your mother's face, you are forced to process the visual information and produce the judgment that it is your mother's face. You do not have the option of not processing the information. Thus, you cannot refuse to produce the judgment that it is your mother's face.

Third, a module is domain-specific as opposed to domain-general. A particular module specializes in processing only a particular kind of information. It does not work on other kinds of information. For example, the face recognition system is devoted to recognizing faces. It only processes the information about faces and nothing else. The theory of mind module is devoted to reading others' minds. So it only processes the information about others' mind and nothing else. A module specializing in interpreting language does not process the information about the shape of a physical object. A module specializing in interpreting a physical object does not process information about language. It is not the case that there is one grand module and that it processes information about faces, others' minds, languages, and physical objects.

Fourth, a module is informationally encapsulated. A module is isolated from other modules. So it is not influenced by the information in other modules. For example, the information contained in the face recognition system does not affect the operation of the theory of mind module, and vice versa. If the information in a module interferes with the operation of another module, the resulting judgment would be different.

Evolutionary theory explains why we have a certain module. In the past, for example, organisms did not have the theory of mind module. So they could not read others' minds. A variation occurred, i.e., some were born with the theory of mind module. The module had a survival and reproductive value in the environment where organisms formed a society and lived together. Organisms without the module died out, and organisms with the module survived and reproduced. The module was passed on to the next generation. It is for this reason that we have the module now. In short, the modular theory of mind sits well with the theory of evolution.

4. Evolutionary Arms Race

An evolutionary arms race is an evolutionary race in which a group of organisms develop adaptations and another group of organisms develop counter-adaptations. This notion casts light on how organisms interacted with each other in their evolutionary histories, how they acquired their features, and how they will evolve in the future. Let me provide some examples.

Cheetahs and gazelles can run fast. How did they acquire such traits? The evolutionary answer goes as follows. In the past, they were slow. A variation occurred to some cheetahs. As a result, they acquired the ability to run faster than other cheetahs. Interestingly, a variation also occurred to some gazelles. As a result, they acquired the ability to run faster than other gazelles. If they had not acquired the capacity, cheetahs would not run as fast as they do today, and vice versa. So it is gazelles that made cheetahs run as fast as they do today, and vice versa. For now, cheetahs are winners in that they can catch gazelles.

A variation, however, may occur to some gazelles in the future. As a result, they may outrun cheetahs. In any event, cheetahs and gazelles have been in an evolutionary arms race with respect to speed.

An evolutionary arms race occurs not only with respect to speed but also with respect to the intensity of poison. For example, a Sierra newt carries neurotoxin in its skin. If a person eats it, death will ensue within 17 minutes. A Sierra garter snake, however, developed resistance to the neurotoxin. How could Sierra newts and Sierra garter snakes acquire such properties? In the past, newts were not venomous, and snakes preyed on newts. A variation occurred to some newts. As a result, they acquired the capacity to store some poison in their skin. Snakes that ate the newts died. A variation, however, also occurred to some snakes. As a result, they acquired the ability to tolerate the poison in the newts' skin. Over successive generations, the intensity of the newts' poison increased, but so did the snakes' ability to resist the poison. For now, the snakes are winners in that they can eat the newts without dying. A variation, however, may occur to some newts in the future. As a result, the intensity of their poison may be so strong that snakes eating them may die immediately. In any event, Sierra newts and Sierra garter snakes have been in an evolutionary arms race with respect to the intensity of poison.

An evolutionary arms race occurs not only between predators and preys but also between hosts and parasites, between humans and germs, between males and females, and between cheaters and cheater-detectors. Cheaters are organisms that deceive other organisms for their own benefits; cheater-detectors are organisms that detect and punish cheaters.

Let me give two examples illustrating the race between cheaters and cheater-detectors. Cuckoos are cheaters in that they deceive wagtails for their own benefit. They lay eggs on wagtails' nests. Wagtails raise cuckoos' chicks, being unable to tell cuckoo chicks from their own chicks. For now, cuckoos are winners in that they successfully take advantage of wagtails. However, wagtails may acquire the ability to distinguish between cuckoo chicks and their own chicks in the future as a result of genetic mutation. To take another example (Park, 2013), psychopaths are cheaters in that they are good at concealing their inner trait. Although they are brutal individuals, they hide their brutal character; they appear to be nice neighbors and intelligent professionals. For now, psychopaths are winners in that non-psychopaths cannot recognize psychopaths just by looking at them. However, non-psychopaths may acquire the ability to identify psychopaths as a result of genetic mutation. In fact, psychopaths' brain waves are different from non-psychopaths' brain waves. Non-psychopaths may acquire the ability to feel the difference between the different brain waves. In any event, evolutionary history is a history of endless battles between cheaters and cheater-detectors.

5. Selfish Gene

Molecular biology, which emerged in the second half of the 20th century, asserts that DNA is responsible for observable characteristics, such as eye color and height. But, more importantly, it is combined with evolutionary biology, explaining why variations occur, and how progeny inherit properties from their parents. Molecular biology says that variations occur due to genetic mutations, and genes are the vehicles for transmitting properties from one generation to the next. In the combined view of molecular biology and evolutionary biology, organisms are the replicators, which make copies of themselves and spread out to the world, and genes provide the means for organisms to evolve.

Richard Dawkins (1976) argues, however, that it is not organisms but genes that evolve and that organisms are merely the means for genes to evolve. Before the appearance of life, there were raw materials on the Earth, such as carbon dioxide, methane, and ammonia.

Sunlight and lightning acted on them. These factors gave rise to replicating molecules, molecules which could make copies of themselves. When they copied themselves, they sometimes made imperfect copies. The erratic copying gave rise to improvements and made evolution possible. These replicating molecules were blind, i.e., they were not conscious, and they did not plan ahead. It is not the case that they evolved toward a goal. These replicating molecules are today called 'genes' or 'DNA molecules.'

What is the relationship between genes and organisms? Genes are to organisms what a driver is to a car. Think about the relationship between a driver and a car. The driver uses the car while it is in good condition. Once it gets old, the driver replaces it with a new one. The same is true of genes and organisms. In the past, there was relentless struggle for existence among genes because there were not enough resources to sustain all of them. Natural selection favored the genes that developed survival machines, which are the organisms that genes built up in cooperation with one another. Some genes got together and become a heart, some eyes, some a hand, and so forth. Genes which formed a survival machine were more likely to survive and reproduce than others which did not make up a survival machine. On this understanding, an organism is simply a temporary vehicle which genes use to survive. Genes use an organism while it is young. Once it grows old, they leap to another body, viz., the old body's offspring. They jump from one organism to another via the means of sex. The old body mates with another old body, allowing for the genes to jump from the old bodies to a young body. So sex is a means for genes to proliferate themselves. Sex also has the function of shuffling different genes. The mixing of different genes facilitates improvement and evolution.

How do genes control the behavior of their survival machines? Genes are to their survival machines as a computer programmer is to a computer. The programmer writes, for example, a chess program. Once the program is set up in the computer, the computer is on its own. The programmer does not give specific instructions on what the computer should do as it plays chess with a human being. The programmer has only given general guidelines on what it should do. Likewise, genes set up a program for their survival machine. Once the program is set up, the survival machine is autonomous. Genes do not give their survival machines specific instructions but only general strategies on how to survive and reproduce. For example, genes instruct human beings to speak language, to have sexual desire, and so on. But they do not instruct human beings to speak Korean, or to have sex with a particular individual at a particular place and at a particular time. The moment-to-moment decisions are made not by the genes but by the survival machine itself.

What is the relationship between genes and the mind? The mind is also a means for genes to propagate themselves. In the past, certain organisms acquired a mind as a result of genetic mutations. They had a better chance to survive and reproduce than those without a mind. Organisms with a mind, for example, formed a mental map of their environment as they explored it with their parents while they were young. So they knew where food and water were. Other organisms did not have a mind, hence did not have such a mental map. When they were hungry, they tried out this or that place in their surroundings. They died of hunger before they found food. As this story suggests, having a mind is advantageous for the survival of an organism. It also gives a reproductive advantage. Genes use our mind as well as our body to proliferate themselves. In that sense, they are selfish.

Dawkins argues that genes are not the sole kind of replicators that go through the evolutionary process. Memes are another kind of replicator. A meme is a distinct memorable unit that evolves by natural selection in our brain or mind. Memes are such things as an idea, a word, a sentence, or a tune. Just as genes leap from a body to another body, so memes leap from one brain to another, or from one mind to another. For genes, sex is the means to leap from a body to another body. For memes, communication provides the means for the leap from one mind to another. On this view, the brain or the mind is the arena in which memes propagate themselves. Memes have the goal of prevailing among as many minds as possible. This explains why painters feel good when people visit their galleries, why singers feel good when people sing their songs, why theists aim to spread their religious beliefs to the world, and why professors wish to produce disciples. From the biological point of view, exhibiting paintings, singing songs, proselytizing nonbelievers, and educating disciples are all attempts for memes to multiply themselves. Therefore, the mind is an arena in which memes survive, reproduce, and die.

Study Questions

1. What are the two central ideas of evolutionary theory? Use these two ideas to explain why we feel pain when our tissue is damaged. How do you respond to the contention that the mind is a product of evolution?

2. Where did moral rule come from? Provide an evolutionary answer to this question. Alternatively, you may respond to the objections to the evolutionary theory that no speciation was observed, that no fossils of intermediate organisms were discovered, that it is unlikely that complex organisms could have been created by chance, and so on.

3. What is prosopagnosia? What is autism? What are the characteristics of modules? How does evolutionary theory explain the existence of the face recognition system and the theory of mind module? Are the answers to these questions agreeable to you?

4. Provide an example of an evolutionary arms race and predict how the organisms in your example will evolve in the future. Are you a cheater or a cheater-detector? Why? What is the relationship between criminals and the police?

5. According to Dawkins, what is the relationship between genes and organisms? How do genes control the behavior of their survival machines? What is the relationship between genes and the mind? Do you agree with Dawkins's answers to these questions?

6. For Dawkins, what is a meme? Define it, and provide an example. Where do memes dwell? How do they multiply themselves? Why does a painter feel frustrated when nobody shows an interest in her painting?

CHAPTER

07

Personal Identity

We believe that the person continues to exist from one time to a later time. For example, John is now a thirty-year-old man. Let's call him Adult John. He was a baby thirty years ago. Let's call him Baby John. Baby John and Adult John look different, behave differently, and do not share memories. Yet, we believe that they are the same individual. What entitles us to this belief? What does it take for a person to persist through time?

These questions are important because the persistence of our personal identities over time grounds our moral and legal responsibilities. Suppose that criminals committed crimes a year ago. Although one year has passed, we believe that they are still blameworthy. We do not believe that they are free from blame because they are different people from the ones who committed the crimes a year ago. We rather believe that they persisted, i.e., that they existing now are the same people as the ones who existed a year ago. But what grounds do we have for believing that a person existing at one point in time is the same person as the one existing at another point in time?

This question triggered philosophers to develop diverse theories of personal identity. They are the psychological approach, the biological approach, the sociological approach, the hybrid approach, and identity nihilism. We will critically examine them in this chapter.

1. The Psychological Approach

1.1. Content

No memories persisted from the time when John was a baby to the time when he is a man. So there is no *direct* psychological connection between Baby John and Adult John. There is, however, an *indirect* psychological connection between them, i.e., they are connected with each other by a series of different memories over time.

Direct vs. Indirect

The psychological connection between the individual at t_1 and the individual at t_5 can be direct or indirect:

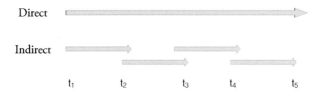

A baby remembers the experience that he had a day ago. So a memory directly connects a baby at t_1 with a baby at t_2. Another memory directly connects the baby at t_2 with the baby at t_3. It follows that Baby John and Adult John are *indirectly* connected with each other, i.e., they are connected with each other by a series of different memories. Since they are psychologically continuous with each other, they are the same individual.

What if there was a temporary interruption, i.e., what if there was a time when John lost all of his memories, but then gained them back?

Psychological Discontinuity

What if John lost all of his memories and gained them back?

Baby John   Adult John

Baby John is psychologically disconnected with Adult John.

If there were such a time, Baby John and Adult John would be psychologically *discontinuous* with each other. They would not even be indirectly connected with each other psychologically. So they would be different individuals according to the psychological approach. The person before he lost memories and the person after he gained his memories back may have similar memories and behave similarly, but they are not the same person.

We can now unpack the psychological approach to personal identity. On the psychological approach, a person at one time is the same as the one at another time insofar as they are psychologically continuous:

> ..identical persons are those who are psychologically continuous with one another. (Schick and Vaughn, 2010: 300-301)

On the psychological approach, some memories must persist for me to maintain my personal identity through time. Thus, what makes me what I am over time is my psychological features. My psychological features constitute my personal identity. If I lost all the psychological features, I would lose my personal identity, i.e., I would cease to be what I am.

Let's apply the psychological approach to some examples. Imagine that after my body dies, my soul goes to heaven, carrying with it some of my memories. Is my soul me or not? The psychological approach says that my soul is me because it is psychologically continuous with me as I was right before my body died.

Suppose that your grandfather suffers from Alzheimer's disease. Is he still your grandfather or a different person? The answer depends on whether he lost all of his memories or not. If he lost all of his memories, he is not your grandfather. After all, he is psychologically discontinuous with your grandfather before he got Alzheimer's disease. In contrast, if at least one memory persists from the time when your grandfather was not stricken with the disease, then he is your grandfather. That memory makes the two individuals existing at different times psychologically continuous.

Suppose that my brain is transplanted into Tom's head. Is the combination of my brain and Tom's body me or Tom? The combination would have most of my memories. So the psychological approach says that he is me. Our intuition also says that he is me. Therefore, the psychological approach is true. Or so it seems.

1.2. Objections

A standard objection to the psychological approach concerns dreamless sleep (Gustafsson, 2011). Do I continue to exist, or cease to exist, when I have a dreamless sleep? On the psychological approach, it looks like I cease to exist. When I am in the dreamless sleep, I do not feel anything. So in the dreamless sleep I am not psychologically continuous with me before the dreamless sleep. Our intuition says, however, that I continue to exist through the dreamless sleep. Since the psychological approach says otherwise, it is false.

Proponents of the psychological approach would admit that I do not have any *conscious* mental state when I am in a dreamless sleep. They would argue, however, that my memories are stored in the *unconscious* realm. So I before the dreamless sleep am psychologically continuous with me after the dreamless sleep by virtue of the memories in the unconscious realm.

Unconscious Realm

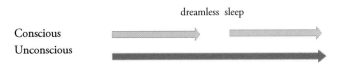

I persist through the dreamless sleep because I maintain psychological features in the unconscious realm.

I before the dreamless sleep am directly connected with me after the dreamless sleep by the unconscious mental states. Therefore, I persist through the dreamless sleep.

Now, consider a bizarre case. A man's brain is transplanted into a woman's head. On the psychological approach, the combination of his brain and her body would be him. After all, the combination is psychologically continuous with him from before the transplantation. It is not clear, though, that the combination is him. She (the combination) looks very different from the man that he was before the transplantation.

If you are not persuaded, consider an even more bizarre case. Suppose that your brain is transplanted into a chimpanzee's head. On the psychological approach, the combination of your brain and the chimpanzee's body would be you. After all, the combination would be psychologically continuous with you from before the transplantation. But it (the combination) would look very different from you as you were before the transplantation.

What if a person were frozen and thawed? On November 11, 2010, an article of Mail Online presents an interesting story about a woman who was frozen and thawed (Reporter: David Gardner). Amy Moore, a thirty-eight-year-old woman in North Carolina, died of a heart attack. Her heart did not beat for twenty minutes. She was pronounced dead by doctors. The doctors froze her, and she was in the frozen state for two days. She was gradually thawed, and came back to life. She talks and behaves as she did before. Is she the same person as the one before she was frozen? The person that she was before she was frozen is psychologically discontinuous with the person that she is after she was thawed. So they are different people on the psychological approach. Our intuition says, however, that they are the same person. Therefore, the psychological approach is false.

2. The Biological Approach

2.1. Content

If your brain is deprived of oxygen for ten minutes, it suffers from irrecoverable damage and you lapse into a vegetative state. There is no chance that you will come back to normal. The organism in the vegetative state cannot think. Nor can it feel pain or emotion. It is a mindless creature.

The psychological approach and the biological approach make different assertions about the identity of a human vegetable. On the psychological approach, the organism in the vegetative state is not you because it is not psychologically continuous with you. You cease to exist the moment you become a human vegetable. In contrast, the biological approach says that the organism is you because it is biologically continuous with you before you fell into the vegetative state. It is biologically continuous with you because its biological functions, such as respiration and blood circulation, have been maintained.

On the biological approach, you persist as long as you maintain some biological functions.

On the biological approach, a person at one time is the same person as the one at another time if and only if they are biologically continuous. You preserve your identity by maintaining your biological functions:

> As long as your body continues to perform its animal functions – respiration, circulation, digestion, and the like – you continue to exist. (Schick and Vaughn, 2010: 272)

Baby John and Adult John are the same person because his biological functions, such as respiration and blood circulation, persisted from the time when he was a baby to the time when he is a man. Metabolism did not stop at any intermediate point in time. If all biological functions had stopped for a moment and then resumed, the baby and the adult would be different individuals. But such an event never occurred. So they are the same individual. Thus, biological continuity enables us to retain our identity over time. Once we lose all biological functions, we lose our identity and cease to be what we are and who we are.

Suppose that my mind is downloaded into a sophisticated computer, so that the computer has all of my memories and talks as if it were me. On the biological approach, the computer is not me because it is not biologically continuous with me. After all, the computer has neither my flesh nor my blood; it has no biological functions at all.

Imagine that after my body dies, my soul is released from my body, and it carries all of my memories. Do I continue to exist or cease to exist? On the biological approach, if my body stops its biological functions, I cease to exist. My living body is biologically discontinuous with my body after it dies. Even if my soul exists and carries all of my memories, my soul is not me because it is not biologically continuous with my body, and I no longer exist. It follows that it is none of my business, but rather the soul's business, whether it goes to heaven or hell.

What if my brain is transplanted into Tom's head? Is the combination of my brain and Tom's body me or Tom? According to the psychological approach, the combination is me because it is psychologically continuous with me. According to the biological approach, however, the combination is both me and Tom, given that my brain in Tom's body is biologically continuous with me, and Tom's body is biologically continuous with Tom.

The biological approach has an advantage over the psychological approach. It can handle the embryo case. Suppose that you are twenty years old and that you were an embryo about twenty years ago. Was the embryo you or not? Our intuition says that it was you. The biological approach also says that it was you on the grounds that it is biologically continuous with you as you are now, i.e., metabolism never stopped in the intermediate point in time. So the embryo and you are the same individual.

2.2. Objections

There are problems with the biological approach. First, the embryo is biologically continuous with the zygote, the combination of a sperm and an egg. The biological approach entails that the zygote was you. But the zygote looks so different from you, and it is nothing but a single cell.

Also, the zygote is biologically continuous with a sperm and an egg in time. The sperm is biologically continuous with a part of your father's body, and the egg is biologically continuous with a part of your mother's body. Therefore, you are biologically continuous with both a part of your father's body and a part of your mother's body. We do not want to say, however, that neither a part of your father's body nor a part of your mother's body was you. Since the biological approach says that they were you, it is false.

What if a person is frozen and thawed? As introduced earlier, Amy Moore was dead for two days and came back to life. Did she persist through the frozen time span? The person before she was frozen is biologically discontinuous with the person after she was thawed. So they are different people on the biological approach. Our intuition says, however, that they are the same person. Therefore, the biological approach is false.

3. The Sociological Approach

Aristotle famously claimed that human beings are social animals. In his spirit, one may propose that a person at one time and a person at another time are the same person if and only if they are sociologically continuous with each other. This view might be called the sociological approach to personal identity. There can be two different versions of the sociological approach, depending on the sociological connection between a person at t_1 and a person t_2. Let me go over them one by one.

On the first version, the sociological connection is the social relations to family members, friends, and the community. Thus, you persist by maintaining those social relations. You are still your mother's son and John's friend, even if you suffer from amnesia, or lapse into a vegetative state. It is not the case that you cease to be your mother's son or John's friend, the moment you get amnesia or fall into a vegetative state. Therefore, you persist through amnesia and the vegetative state.

The first version of the sociological approach has the following problem. What if you lose all of your social relations? Imagine that World War III occurs and that everyone dies except you. You are alone in the world. Even so, you would continue to be you. It is not the case that you would cease to exist, and become a different person the moment you lose all of your social relations. So says our intuition. The first version of the sociological approach says, however, that you would lose your personal identity, and you would no longer be you as you were before. Therefore, the first version is false.

On the second version of the sociological approach, the sociological connection inheres in people's beliefs. Specifically, John at t_1 is the same person as John at t_2 because people around him maintain their belief that they are the same person. Suppose, for example, that your grandfather suffers from Alzheimer's disease. He persists so long as people around him continue to think of him as your grandfather. To take another example, even if you fall into a vegetative state, you continue to exist insofar as people around you continue to think of the human vegetable as you. Thus, Baby John and Adult John are the same person because they are sociologically continuous with each other, i.e., because people around Baby John and Adult John retain their belief that Baby John and Adult John are the same person. Thus, sociological continuity makes it possible for people to preserve their identities through time.

The second version of the sociological approach has the following problems: First, what if the half of your family members think of the human vegetable as you, but the other half of your family members do not think of the human vegetable as you? It is a contradiction to say that the human vegetable is both you and not you. Second, what if you are on a desert island alone and everyone forgets you? Do you continue to exist? On the sociological approach, you no longer exist because no one believes that you do. Our intuition says, however, that you continue to exist. Therefore, the sociological approach is false.

4. The Hybrid Approach

The hybrid approach states that a person persists by maintaining psychological, biological, or sociological features. I persist, for example, even if I suffer from amnesia because my bodily functions are maintained. Amnesia causes a psychological discontinuity, but not a biological one. I also persist, for example, even if my mind were downloaded into a sophisticated computer because my mental features are maintained in the computer. Downloading my mind into the computer would create a biological discontinuity, but not a psychological one.

On the hybrid approach, what makes me what I am are my mental, bodily, or social features.

The Hybrid Approach

I persist by maintaining my mental, bodily, or social features.

t₁   t₂   t₃   t₄

The person at t_1 and the person at t_2 are connected by biological features. The person at t_2 and the person at t_3 are connected by psychological features. The person at t_3 and the person at t_4 are connected by sociological features. Thus, there is an indirect connection between the person at t_1 and the person at t_4. Hence, they are the same person. On the hybrid approach, people cease to exist, only when they lose all three sets of features entirely.

There are problems with the hybrid approach. What if my mind is downloaded into a computer and my body becomes mindless? On the hybrid approach, I exist in the computer because it is psychologically continuous with me, and I also exist in the mindless body because it is biologically continuous with me. But how can I exist in two different places (in the computer and in the mindless body) at the same time?

Moreover, what if you die, but your family members continue to think of your body as you? The hybrid approach says that the body is you because it is sociologically continuous with you before you die. Our intuition says, however, that your body is not you. Therefore, the hybrid approach is false.

Realizing that sociological continuity causes trouble for the hybrid approach, proponents of the hybrid approach may propose a new version according to which a person persists when there is either psychological or biological continuity through time. Note that sociological continuity does not figure in this new account.

There are still problems with this new version of the hybrid approach. What if a person is frozen and thawed? There is neither psychological nor biological continuity. But our intuition says that the person persists. Moreover, suppose that my mind is downloaded into an advanced computer and that my body becomes free of my mind. My mind is psychologically continuous with the computer, and my body is biologically continuous with itself. It follows that according to this new version, both the computer and the body are me. But how can I be both the computer and the body?

5. Identity Nihilism

All four approaches to personal identity – the psychological, biological, sociological, and hybrid approach – have problems. It is not clear what grounds we have for believing that a person at one time is the same as the person at another time. In the face of this gloomy situation, one might despair and embrace what I call identity nihilism. Identity nihilism asserts that identity is an illusion. As time passes, people become different individuals. We just think that they maintain their identities through time when, in fact, they do not. Strictly speaking, Baby John and Adult John are different individuals, although we think that they are the same individual. We only use the same name 'John' to refer to the two people existing at different times because it is convenient to do so.

Identity nihilism is not an absurd position. Heraclitus, an ancient Greek philosopher, would be happy to embrace it. He famously claimed that everything changes and that you cannot "step into the same river twice" (Jones, 1970: 16). Taehwa River, for example, runs through Ulsan City in South Korea. Suppose that you stepped into the river at t_1 and t_2. You may think that you stepped into the same river twice. Strictly speaking, however, the river at t_1 and the river at t_2 are different rivers because they were composed of different waters. So you actually stepped into two different rivers. So claims Heraclitus.

A problem with identity nihilism is that it has the absurd consequence that we ought not to punish criminals for the crimes that they committed. On the nihilist view, as time passes, criminals lose their identities and become different individuals. So those locked up in prison are not the ones who committed crimes in the past. The ones who committed crimes in the past no longer exist. Therefore, it is wrong to punish the inmates. Our intuition says, however, that the inmates are the very individuals who committed the crimes in the past. Therefore, the inmates are reprehensible and should be held accountable for their past actions. Since identity nihilism says otherwise, it is false. Thus, we are back to our original question: On what grounds can we say that a person persists over time?

Study Questions

1. What if my body dies and my soul is released from it? What if your grandfather suffers from Alzheimer's disease? What if my brain is transplanted into Tom's head? Answer these questions

from the perspective of the psychological approach and evaluate your answers.

2. What if my mind is downloaded into a sophisticated computer? What if a person suffers from multiple personality disorder? What if I commit crime, my brain is cut in halves, and they are transplanted into two different people? Who should be punished? Answer these questions from the viewpoint of the psychological approach and appraise your answers.

3. Are identical twins the same individual or different individuals? How about me and my clone? Answers these questions from the perspective of the biological approach and assess your answers.

4. What if my body is divided into many pieces and they are transplanted into many different people? What if I received different organs from different people? Answer these questions from the point of view of the biological approach and appraise them.

5. State the sociological approach, the hybrid approach, and identity nihilism. Are they defensible?

6. Imagine that a person committed a crime a year ago, the criminal

is tried in court, and you are a judge. A lawyer claims that the defendant is innocent because the past criminal and the defendant are different individuals. On what grounds would you punish the defendant? Which approach to personal identity would you take?

References

Aquinas, St. Thomas (1975). *Summa Theologiae*. Latin text, English translation, Introduction, Notes, Appendices, and Glossary by Marcus Lefebure, London and New York: Blackfriars and McGraw-Hill.

Arthur, John (1996). "Religion, Morality, and Conscience," In John Arthur, (ed.), *Morality and Moral Controversies*. 4thed.,PrenticeHall.

Boethius (1962). *The Consolation of Philosophy*. prose VII, trans. Richard Green, New York: The Bobbs-Merrill Company, Inc.

Churchland, Patricia (1997). "Can Neurobiology Teach Us Anything about Consciousness?", In Ned Block, Owen Flanagan, and Güven Güzeldere (eds.), *The Nature of Consciousness*. Cambridge, MA: MIT Press.

Copi, Iirving and Carl Cohen (2009). *Introduction to Logic*. 13 ed., Upper Saddle River, New Jersey: Pearson Education, Inc.

Crick, Francis (1994). *The Astonishing Hypothesis*. New York: Simon and Schuster.

Dawkins, Richard (1976). *The Selfish Gene*. USA: Oxford University Press.

Elisabeth of Bohemia (1643/1994). "Letters to Descartes" In *Women Philosophers of the Early Modern Period*. Atherton, M. (ed.), (1994), Hackett Publishing Company.

Feldman, Fred (1992). *Confrontations with the Reaper: A Philosophical Study of the Nature and Value of Death*. Oxford: Oxford University Press.

Goldman, Alvin (1979). "What is Justified Belief?" In George Pappas, (ed.), *Justification and Knowledge*. Kluwer Academic Publisher.

---------- (1993). "The Psychology of Folk Psychology," *Behavioral and Brain Sciences* 16: 15-28.

---------- (1999). *Knowledge in a Social World*. Oxford: Oxford University Press.

Gustafsson, Johan E. (2011). "Phenomenal Continuity and the Bridge Problem", *Philosophia* 39 (2): 289-296.

Hare, Richard (1970). *Freedom and Reason*. London: Oxford University

Press.

Harman, Gilbert (2008). "Moral Relativism" In Satris, Stephen (ed.), *Taking Sides: Clashing Views on Moral Issues*. (10[th]ed.)Mcgraw-HillCompanies.

Hick, John (1966). *Evil and the God of Love*. New York: Harper and Tow.

Hume, David (1779/1947). *Dialogues Concerning Natural Religion*. Norman K. Smith (ed.), Indianapolis: Bobbs-Merrill.

---------- (1888/1978). *Treatise of Human Nature*. L. Selby and P. Nidditch (eds.), USA: Oxford University Press.

Huxley, Thomas (1893). *Method and Results*. New York: Appleton-Century-Crofts.

Jones, T. W. (1970). *A History of Western Philosophy: The Classical Mind*. Fort Worth: Harcourt Brace Jovanovich.

Kant, Immanuel (1785/2011). *Groundwork of the Metaphysics of Morals*. Jens Timmermann (ed.), New York: Cambridge University Press.

Kitcher, Philip (1982). *Abusing Science: The Case against Creationism*. Cambridge, MA: The MIT Press.

Layman, Stephen (1991). "Ethics and the Kingdom of God", In Stephen Satris (ed.), (2008). *Taking Sides: Clashing Views on Moral Issues*. 11[th]ed.Mcgraw-Hill/Dushkin.

Lewis, David (1980). "Mad Pain and Martian Pain", in *Readings in Philosophy of Psychology*. In Block, N. (ed.), Cambridge: Harvard University Press.

Libet, Benjamin (1985). "Unconscious Cerebral Initiative and the Role of Conscious Will in Voluntary Action", *The Behavioral and Brain Sciences* 8 (4): 529–566.

Mackie, John (1977). *Ethics: Inventing Right and Wrong*. Harmondsworth: Middlesex.

Moser, Paul, Dwayne Mulder, and J. D. Trout (1998). *The Theory of Knowledge: A Thematic Introduction*. New York: Oxford University Press.

Nagel, Thomas (1974). "What Is It Like to Be a Bat?", *Philosophical Review* 83 (4): 435-450.

Park, Seungbae (2013). "Evolutionary Explanation of Psychopaths", *International Journal of Social Science Studies* 1 (2): 1-7.

---------- (2016). "Extensional Scientific Realism vs. Intensional Scientific Realism," *Studies in History and Philosophy of Science* 59: 46-52.

Ockham, William (1983). *Predestination, God's Foreknowledge, and Future Contingents*. Indianapolis: Hackett Publishing Company.

Putnam, Hillary (1967/1975). "Psychological Predicates", In *Mind, Language, and Reality: Philosophical Papers*. (1975), vol. 2, Cambridge: Cambridge University Press.

---------- (1975). *Mind, Language, and Reality, Philosophical Papers*. vo. 2 London: Cambridge University Press.

---------- (1981). *Reason, Truth and History*. Cambridge: Cambridge University Press.

Quine, Willard, V. O. (1994). *From a Logical Point of View: Nine Logico-Philosophical Essays*. Cambridge: Harvard University Press.

Rawls, John (1971). *A Theory of Justice*. Cambridge: Harvard University Press.

Schick, Theodore Jr. and Lewis Vaughn (2010). *Doing Philosophy: An Introduction through Thought Experiments*. 3rd ed., New York, NY: The McGraw-Hill Companies.

Sherman, Paul W. and Samuel M. Flaxman (2002). "Nausea and Vomiting of Pregnancy in an Evolutionary Perspective", *American Journal of Obstetrics and Gynecology* 186 (suppl.): S190-197.

Smart, J. J. C. (1959). "Sensations and Brain Processes", *Philosophical Review* 68: 141-156.

Sober, Elliot (1993). *Philosophy of Biology*. Colorado: Westview Press.

Wykstra, Stephen J. (1984). "The Humean Obstacle to Evidential Arguments from Suffering: On Avoiding the Evils of Appearance," *International Journal for the Philosophy of Religion* 16 (2): 73-93.

Index

박승배 (Seungbae Park)

Seungbae Park is Associate Professor of Philosophy at Ulsan National Institute of Science and Technology in the Republic of Korea. He received his Ph.D. from the University of Arizona in 2001, having specialized in philosophy of science under the guidance of Prof. Richard Healey. He taught at the University of Arizona, the University of Maryland, and POSTECH, before coming to his current institution in 2009. He has published papers in Studies in History and Philosophy of Science, Creativity Studies, Acta Analytica, Philosophia, Foundations of Science, Axiomathes, Filosofija.Sociologija, European Journal of Science and Theology, Journal for General Philosophy of Science, Philosophical Papers, and so forth.

Great Debates
in Philosophy

초판인쇄 2016년 11월 18일
초판발행 2016년 11월 18일

지은이 박승배(Seungbae Park)
펴낸이 채종준
펴낸곳 한국학술정보㈜
주소 경기도 파주시 회동길 230(문발동)
전화 031) 908-3181(대표)
팩스 031) 908-3189
홈페이지 http://ebook.kstudy.com
전자우편 출판사업부 publish@kstudy.com
등록 제일산-115호(2000. 6. 19)

ISBN 978-89-268-7622-0 93160

이 책은 한국학술정보㈜와 저작자의 지적 재산으로서 무단 전제와 복제를 금합니다.
책에 대한 더 나은 생각, 끊임없는 고민, 독자를 생각하는 마음으로 보다 좋은 책을 만들어갑니다.